D0677872

JUN 1 7 2016

# THE RETIREMENT RESCUE PLAN

Copyright © 2016 by Melissa Phipps

No part of this publication may be reproduced, stored in a retrieval system or transmitted in any form or by any means, electronic, mechanical, photocopying, recording, scanning or otherwise, except as permitted under Sections 107 or 108 of the 1976 United States Copyright Act, without the prior written permission of the Publisher. Requests to the Publisher for permission should be addressed to the Permissions Department, Sonoma Press, 918 Parker St, Suite A-12, Berkeley, CA 94710.

Limit of Liability/Disclaimer of Warranty: The Publisher and the author make no representations or warranties with respect to the accuracy or completeness of the contents of this work and specifically disclaim all warranties, including without limitation warranties of fitness for a particular purpose. No warranty may be created or extended by sales or promotional materials. The advice and strategies contained herein may not be suitable for every situation. This work is sold with the understanding that the Publisher is not engaged in rendering medical, legal or other professional advice or services. If professional assistance is required, the services of a competent professional person should be sought. Neither the Publisher nor the author shall be liable for damages arising herefrom. The fact that an individual, organization or website is referred to in this work as a citation and/or potential source of further information does not mean that the author or the Publisher endorses the information the individual, organization or website may provide or recommendations they/it may make. Further, readers should be aware that Internet websites listed in this work may have changed or disappeared between when this work was written and when it is read.

For general information on our other products and services or to obtain technical support, please contact our Customer Care Department within the U.S. at (866) 744-2665, or outside the U.S. at (510) 253-0500.

Sonoma Press publishes its books in a variety of electronic and print formats. Some content that appears in print may not be available in electronic books, and vice versa.

TRADEMARKS: Sonoma Press and the Sonoma Press logo are trademarks or registered trademarks of Callisto Media Inc. and/or its affiliates, in the United States and other countries, and may not be used without written permission. All other trademarks are the property of their respective owners. Sonoma Press is not associated with any product or vendor mentioned in this book.

ISBN: Print 978-1-943451-22-7 | eBook 978-1-943451-23-4

# THE
# RETIREMENT
# RESCUE PLAN

Retirement Planning Solutions
for the Millions of Americans
Who Haven't Saved "Enough"

## MELISSA PHIPPS

**SONOMA
PRESS**

INDIAN PRAIRIE PUBLIC LIBRARY
401 Plainfield Rd
Darien, IL 60561

# Contents

# Foreword

**I was a bit skeptical** when Melissa Phipps first asked me to look over *The Retirement Rescue Plan*. As a writer who covers second-act careers, I routinely read more than my fair share of books about retirement, and quite frankly, most are predictable, formulaic, and alarmist in nature.

Turns out I was wrong to be concerned. This book really *does* offer fresh, realistic, and comprehensive solutions for the millions of Americans who haven't saved enough for retirement.

And if that describes you, you've picked up the right book.

*The Retirement Rescue Plan* is an important read because retirement as we know it is rapidly changing. Not so very long ago, most of us expected to enjoy a leisure-based retirement of golfing, gardening, and shuffleboard—supported by a pension, Social Security, and a bit of savings too.

Today, that retirement model is all but gone. Increasingly long lifespans have created what experts term a "longevity bonus"—an extra thirty years or so when most of us can expect to be productive and engaged in the world.

But while that is welcome news, there is also a serious financial downside to the longevity bonus. Few of us are eligible for employer-sponsored pensions, and it has become increasingly difficult to sock away enough for a lengthy retirement. Even for those of us who save regularly, the combination of swings in the stock market, historically low interest rates, spiraling health care costs, and uncertainty about the stability of Social Security adds a dangerous amount of volatility to the mix.

As a result, a new paradigm of retirement—or "unretirement"—has emerged. Multiple surveys indicate that a majority of boomers expect to work past traditional retirement age. Of course, this doesn't mean that they want to work in the same way, doing the same things, at the same dizzying pace, that they've maintained while employed full-time.

Instead, they are pursuing a variety of entrepreneurial ventures, volunteer assignments, and new careers that allow them to work on their own terms and on their own timetable. They are finding meaning and purpose in retirement—while still having enough time and money to enjoy family, travel, and personal pursuits.

If that's what you want, too, then Melissa's book is a welcome guide that will help you craft a personalized retirement plan that is built around *your* unique needs and dreams.

This process won't be simple or quick. As a career coach with over 20 years of experience helping people navigate challenging transitions, I know all too well that change is a messy and sometimes painful process. You might need to make adjustments to your spending and your lifestyle. That is rarely easy.

But as you work through the exercises in this book, you'll be amazed at how quickly you gain a sense of control over your future. *The Retirement Rescue Plan* features a step-by-step plan to help you assess your current financial reality, determine what really matters to you in life, brainstorm options for generating income, and retire your own way.

Best of all, *The Retirement Rescue Plan* will stimulate you to think in new directions, see possibilities you might not have considered, and motivate you to make positive changes in your life.

In short, it will ease your worries and give you hope for the future.

Read it, learn from it, and then go plan your happy, secure, and fulfilling retirement. The time to begin is now.

NANCY COLLAMER
MyLifestyleCareer.com
Author, *Second-Act Careers*

# Preface

**"The time is now."** This is what I said to myself on my last day working for someone else. I had been at the same job for years, working on a career track that was no longer as defined as it had once seemed, fighting to find ways to be passionate about a job that had become routine. We've all been there, right? It seems to be a pretty common story these days.

That day, I faced a decision: accept a new job under a restructure or take a layoff. The restructure would be more of the same unfulfilling work, at a job bearing no resemblance to what I'd set out to do, which was simply to help people better understand their money. It was a variation on a theme: I'd spent the previous 15 years working as a writer and editor at magazines and websites, and each job looked nothing like the one before. I was at least 25 years from traditional retirement age and knew I would have to continue to work. But I was ready for a change. "The time is now," I thought when I quit my 9-to-5 job and went into business for myself.

It wasn't exactly retirement, but it was an important first step. In the years I've spent working as a personal finance journalist, retirement has been one of my favorite subjects to talk about. Not because I love annual 401(k) plan contribution limits, or because I go gaga over complicated Roth IRA withdrawal rules. Don't get me wrong; I appreciate a good tax-advantaged retirement account, and you should be stuffing extra money in yours as early and as often as you can. But where to save and how much to save are not as interesting to me as *why* we save.

To me, the notion of retirement is kind of like the modern American dream. It's the promise that if you work hard enough, you can enjoy an idealized future when there will be more time to spend with your friends and family, engage in your favorite hobbies, indulge your whims and passions—more time to do what you always wanted to do, before your job got in the way.

Like the American dream, the traditional, secure retirement that I was brought up to believe in is harder to come by these days. I think there are several reasons for this. For one thing, Americans are living longer lives. The employer pensions that sustained the post-working lives of our parents and grandparents are scarce. Jobs generally don't offer the security of sustained employment throughout your career. Even our investments seem less cooperative than they did a few decades ago. For today's retirees, bonds are no sure source of income, stocks can swing wildly, and safe havens for your investments are hard to come by. A plan to retire at age 67 could be derailed by a layoff or a market crash. Or it can keep workers like me in miserable jobs for longer than necessary because the promise of retiring to a golf course is the only option.

But in a way, that's okay. I've made my peace with it. Because the tradeoff for losing out on a routine retirement is that we don't all have to retire in the same way. Advances in technology and communication and the rise of the gig economy make it easier than ever for people to redefine their own work lives and to leave the workforce gradually. Retirement today looks different depending on who you talk to. For some people it's about working less or going into business for themselves; for others it's about doing something meaningful through a nonprofit or volunteer work. It's rarely about doing nothing at all.

Once you embrace the new retirement reality, you can make the most of it. Sure, there's uncertainty, but with uncertainty comes flexibility, even opportunity. That's why I've written this book: to encourage you to see the possibilities in today's retirement challenges.

Retirement today requires a shift in perspective. It's a chance to change your routine and make more time for the things you enjoy. But it doesn't necessarily mean that you stop working—and that's a good thing. It's likely that you will live longer than your parents and grandparents did, so it makes sense that you will work longer, too. A little bit of work keeps you social, active, and sharp. Plenty of vibrant people living in their 50s, 60s, and 70s prefer to keep contributing to their communities. Today's retirement encourages that.

It's never too late to plan for retirement, but you do need a plan, which is what I lacked on the day I quit my 9-to-5 job. I acted spontaneously, before laying the groundwork that would allow me to be successful. I took on too much work and became more stressed than ever. Because times seemed flush, I didn't budget my expenses. I didn't purchase life insurance or disability insurance to protect my business in case there were bad years. I knew all of these things were important—I'd written countless articles warning people of the risks—yet I was too busy to think about them.

It took me years to realize that my lack of planning had set me up to fail, and that only happened after breast cancer came along and took a bite out of my productivity. During months of chemotherapy and radiation, I thought a lot about what I wanted in life, about what truly makes me happy, and about what I would do differently if there were still time. And then there was time. So I rebuilt. I re-prioritized things in my life, refocused my thinking, and found new work and more interesting opportunities. I got smart about savings and insurance. I developed contingency plans.

Like many retirees, I learned the importance of planning the hard way. The upside is that I have some valuable lessons to share with people like you, who want to retire but don't think it's possible. I want to help you see the potential in the new retirement, to know what you want and develop a plan to get it, to work less, earn enough, and be happier than ever.

You can start today, if you decide to take this adventure with me.

# Never Too Late

**You can retire.** Even if you haven't planned enough, or you worry that you haven't saved enough, it's not too late to create a retirement plan that allows you to quit the 9-to-5 life and live comfortably; earning enough to meet your needs, with a little extra socked away for emergencies. Whether you are a few birthdays or a few decades away from traditional retirement age, you *can* create a plan that will allow you to spend more time relaxing and doing what you love.

I know you've been told this is impossible. The media routinely send the message that Americans are unprepared for retirement, citing dire statistics. Nearly two-thirds of workers report feeling behind schedule when it comes to planning and saving for retirement.[1] The rest of the population are apparently either completely ready or completely oblivious. According to one recent *Money* magazine article: "When it comes to saving for retirement, most American workers are not only falling short, they don't even know how behind they are."[2]

Here's the thing: We're aware. We're not stupid. We're just unprepared.

Now, I'm sure there are some people who feel like their retirement is already taken care of. If you are one of those people who have invested well in a career, a portfolio, or a trust fund, and who could drop out of the workforce on a moment's notice without feeling a pinch, I'm impressed, and maybe a little envious, but this book is not for the one-quarter of American workers who are confident they will be financially secure in retirement.[3] This book is for the rest of us. Those of us who have gotten a late start, who haven't planned or saved enough, who are underprepared, but want to retire anyway. And, yes, we can.

# A Plan for the Retirement Challenged

Saving adequately for retirement is not the only problem. We may have waited a few years before finding out what the 401(k) thing is about, or skipped contributing to an IRA for a year or two when the budget was tight, but most of us have something saved for the future. According to data from the Federal Reserve, the median value of retirement accounts is around $148,900 for Americans ages 65 to 74, and $103,200 for Americans ages 55 to 64.[4]

The problem lies partly with the assumption about what retirement should be. The idea of retirement was born in a time when a guy worked at the same company until age 65 and left with a gold watch and a full-salary pension to spend his days playing golf until dying at age 68. This guy also probably spent his career in an office stocked with full bars and full ashtrays, and referred to his secretary as "doll." That's how antiquated our notion of retirement is.

While the idea of retirement has not evolved much since the *Mad Men* generation of the 1960s, the reality of retirement has changed dramatically. For one thing, we're living longer. A man who reaches age 65 today has a 50 percent chance of living at least 17 more years, to age 82. A 65-year-old woman has the same chance of living 20 more years, to age 85, and a 28 percent chance of living past 90. That's a lot of potential years to fund if you aren't working. Meanwhile, the burden of funding those years has shifted from the employer to the employee. Only about 14 percent of private sector workers participate in a traditional benefit pension that guarantees income in retirement, according to the Employee Benefits Research Institute.[5] Social Security is guaranteed, but is designed as a supplementary benefit, about 40 percent of the income a person earned with full-time work.[6]

The idea that the average worker can save enough during her career to replace 60 percent of her income for 20 years or more is not always realistic. Even if you are a diligent saver and have done everything right, a volatile stock market or health issues could derail your plan. You may have to live during retirement on a reduced income or risk running out of money.

# The New Work-Retirement Balance

Money aside, having decades of free time isn't necessarily an attractive option, either. That's what I hear from the retirees from across the country whom I have surveyed or interviewed for this book. Retirees who told me stories of successful and often gradual retirements. These people spend time in retirement working as teachers, or bloggers, or home investors and remodelers. One woman, who was miserable in the final years of her job, found a sense of joyous vengeance in coming back as a consultant after retirement, earning more income in her new, carefree role than she had in decades with the company. These are people who, for the most part, are engaged in work or volunteering, usually for the income, but also for the sense of purpose and accomplishment that comes with staying involved with the world and doing something meaningful. Throughout this book I share some of their quotes, stories, and tips. Most say they are happily retired, but not ready for a life without daily purpose and tasks.

On a national level, a growing number of seniors are choosing to continue working or go back to work after retirement. The number of Americans ages 65 to 74 in the workforce has more than doubled since 1990, and that demographic is projected by the Bureau of Labor Statistics to represent nearly 32 percent of total workers by 2022.[7] A recent Reuters-Ipsos survey of more than 7,700 adults found that, among the retired respondents, 30 percent said they would "unretire" if a job became available.[8]

These days, more people hope to transition into retirement by gradually shifting into part-time or consulting roles before stopping work completely. Entrepreneurship is up among the 50-plus set, and more seniors are getting involved in the gig economy through businesses like Uber, Airbnb, TaskRabbit, and eBay.[9] In short, there are plenty of opportunities for those who want to leave the 9-to-5 world.

As the following table shows, less than 22 percent of would-be retirees who responded to a survey, issued by the Federal Reserve, plan to go the traditional route of stopping working altogether.

## TABLE 1 **PATHS VARY FOR WOULD-BE RETIREES**

In its annual survey of American households, the Federal Reserve asked nearly 3,900 nonretired or disabled respondents which of the following best describes their plan for retirement:

| | |
|---|---|
| Keep working as long as possible | 26.5% |
| Work full-time until I retire, then stop working altogether | 21.6% |
| Retire from my career, then find a different part-time job | 12.5% |
| I do not plan to retire | 11.5% |
| Work fewer hours in retirement | 9.3% |
| Retire from my career, then go work for myself | 8.1% |
| Retire from my career, then find a different full-time job | 2.6% |

*Source: Federal Reserve 2015*

What I am going to suggest throughout this book is, if you are nearing retirement with little savings or big gaps in retirement income, the best solution is part-time work or consider switching to another line of work.

# Work Less, Earn Enough, Be Happier Than Ever

I want you to feel prepared to retire in a way that takes *you* into account—your desires, abilities, needs, and actual savings. Research finds that having a sense of control over how and when you retire, and taking steps beforehand to build the kind of retirement you want, is by itself likely to improve the retirement experience.[10] This book is designed to help you build a realistic retirement plan, and quickly.

Make no mistake, with this plan you can work less. But you will likely have to work at least part of the time. Why not envision doing something fun and interesting? What did you always want to do before the day job got in the way? It's not too late to share your passions and talents with the world, to try something completely new.

Or you may want to focus on doing whatever provides the easiest path to doing nothing. This book will show you how to ease into retirement at your own pace and how to spend more time—both professionally and recreationally—doing what you enjoy.

In terms of savings, I want you to stop worrying about whether what you have is enough, and focus instead on how to make the most of what you have. Now is the time to find and maximize opportunities for future income and savings.

Because you are making up for lost time, the process I will take you through in this book will not be painless. You need to be honest with yourself about your expenses. There will be budgeting, and you may have to adjust your lifestyle or expectations if you want to make your budget work.

There will also be a certain amount of navel gazing. You will have to think deeply about what really makes you happy, what you'd want to do if you could do anything at all.

Then, you'll put your plan in motion. In part 1, you will diagram what's most meaningful to you; in part 2, you will figure out where you can earn additional income; and in part 3, you will start practicing for life in retirement. The information, worksheets, and quizzes in this book are designed to help you determine where you stand now, where you want to be, and which milestones you need to focus on to retire as happily as you'd always hoped, much sooner than you expected.

It's never too late to plan a happy retirement. This book will help you envision, create, and commit to a path that will bring you to the life you desire.

Yes, you really can!

# 1

# WORK LESS

The new retirement is all about working less and finding more time for happiness. The first question to consider is the most crucial one: What makes you happy? Most people will find that day-to-day happiness comes from something other than money. In this section, I'll help you define what happiness looks like for you.

But we'll also talk about money, because money can either enable you to do the things that make you happy, or it can hold you back. In part 1, I will help you take inventory of your financial situation. You'll get a sense of how your savings can be turned into income, and how to maximize your Social Security, pensions, and investment accounts. This is all necessary to retire. The goal is to develop an overview of your retirement expenses and a budget that fits your retirement lifestyle.

# Part 1 Milestones

1.  Determine what really matters to you and the steps you need to take to lead a happier life.

2.  Get serious about your finances. Figure out how much income you can generate in retirement.

3.  Map out exactly what you can expect from Social Security, retirement accounts, pension, and taxable investments.

4.  Estimate future expenses and needs.

5.  Calculate a realistic budget that helps you find your happiness.

It's a lot, I know! But these five steps will help you lay the groundwork for your retirement. There's no time to waste, so let's get started.

# CHAPTER
# ONE

# What Makes You Happy?

Before we get into the financial aspect of retirement, I want to explore an even more complicated and elusive subject: happiness.

Happiness is a tricky word, isn't it? Is it a singular concept or something more elastic? Is it a state of constant joy or pleasure? A release from everyday worries? Is happiness a by-product of big events or is it found in simple indulgences—a chocolate bar, a well-liked Facebook post, a room upgrade on vacation? Or is it a sense of purpose and fulfillment, a sense of doing what you were meant to do?

So bear with me. In this chapter I'm going to use some basic questions and proven techniques to find out what makes you happy. Then we'll be able to build a retirement plan that makes sense for you.

# The Happiness Question

As you can tell, happiness is an unwieldy topic. Perhaps it's because there is no correct response to the happiness question—it's completely subjective. Or maybe the problem is that it requires a level of self-examination that so many of us don't have the time for in today's fast-paced world.

Nobel Prize–winning behavioral economist and psychologist Daniel Kahneman put it best in the book *Well-Being: Foundations of Hedonic Psychology*: "People have ready-made answers to many questions about themselves; they know their name, their address, and their party affiliation. But they do not generally know how happy they are, and they must construct an answer to that question, whenever it is raised."

Kahneman distinguished between two types of happiness: everyday contentment, or emotional well-being; and life assessment, or "the thoughts people have about their life when they think about it." Everyday well-being comes from our experience of emotions such as joy, pleasure, and contentment. Life assessment is based on more tangible measurements, like receiving a promotion or feeling comfortable in your home.

Further confusing things is that when we think about our life it's easy to compare ourselves to others. Do we have as much money as our friends and neighbors, a house as big and beautiful, a car as sleek and shiny? Are our accomplishments on par? Social comparisons are completely normal and perhaps unavoidable. They may even make you feel good, if the comparisons are favorable to you. But they are not likely to help you understand your own happiness.

Even if you don't spend a lot of time keeping up with the proverbial Joneses, happiness can also be confused with momentum. It's easy to spend a career striving for the next level of achievement or attainment, without even thinking about whether each move is what you really want.

You might instead downplay your personal happiness or put it on hold until you've reached a certain goal. As a parent, for example, once my first child was born, I generally stopped making my own

> I feel like I am standing in front of a huge smorgasbord of activities, similar to the grand buffet at the Palace Hotel in San Francisco in the 1950s adorned with many fine delicacies of gourmet delights. I remember the dessert table so well with whipped cream in many colors and shapes added to mini cakes and pastries. So many choices. Then it was food; now it is life . . . the rest of my life.
>
> JUDIE BLOCK, RETIRED IN SANTA CRUZ[11]

happiness a priority. What makes me happy besides the well-being of my kids? I had to give that some serious thought.

Retirement is full of free time. You want to spend it doing what you enjoy. And if you have to continue working because your retirement savings have come up short, you might as well do something you really love. Consider how you want your life to look when you reflect back on it. What can you do that will make you feel good about yourself as a person in the world?

For some people, looking for more meaningful work has become a sort of modern day, late-mid-life crisis. A study of large-company employees ages 50 and older, conducted by the Sloan Center on Aging & Work at Boston College, found that people ranked "opportunities for meaningful work" higher in importance than pay and benefits.[12] According to the nonprofit group Encore.org, there are currently upwards of 4.5 million Americans ages 50 to 70 years, giving back, by engaging in "encore" or second-act careers that address social needs. Another 25 million people plan to do the same.[13]

Maybe you know exactly what you'd do if you had nothing but "me time." On the other hand, if you find it challenging to come up with something, the exercises in this chapter can help. They are designed to get your creative mojo working, so please silence your inner critic and really engage with the exercises. I promise, no one is grading you and you don't have to show your work.

S cholars, scientists and behavioral researchers have been asking themselves for millennia what makes people happy. The Greek philosopher Aristotle gave more thought to happiness than most. In his *Nicomachean Ethics*, originally published in 350 BC, Aristotle posited that happiness lies within a goal that we choose for its own sake, rather than as a means to an end. That still rings very true to me, but recent studies have become even more specific about what makes us happy in the modern age.

### ✦ SPENDING TIME WITH FRIENDS & FAMILY

Strong social relationships are what distinguish the happiest 10 percent of the population, according to Harvard University professor Shawn Achor in his book, *The Happiness Advantage*.[14] Similar research has found that being cared for by friends and relatives—and caring for them in return—can lead to a longer, more fulfilled life.[15]

### ✦ UTILIZING TALENT & SKILL

Doing something you are good at is as satisfying as doing something you love. Achor's research also found that people who were asked to use their signature strengths, or the things they are uniquely talented at, on a daily basis were significantly happier for months afterward.

CONTINUED ▸▸

## ✈ STAYING BUSY WITH PURPOSE

Having nothing to do may sound like the ideal, but long-term studies done by sociologist John P. Robinson at the University of Maryland find that people are more satisfied when they are busy, but not rushed.[16]

## ✈ HAVING JUST ENOUGH MONEY

The old adage, "money can't buy happiness," is wrong—up to a point. A popular 2010 study by Daniel Kahneman and economist Angus Deaton found that the level of happiness money can buy plateaus at around $75,000 a year. Having an annual income higher than that does not increase a person's day-to-day emotional well-being. More recently, that benchmark has been adjusted for each of the 50 states in America, with the happiness threshold of New Yorkers closer to $99,000, for example, and Iowans plateauing at just more than $69,000,[17] but the point is still clear. While having a higher income can decrease your level of sadness, it doesn't necessarily increase your happiness.[18]

## ✈ FAVORING EXPERIENCES OVER THINGS

If you are going to try and buy happiness, a significant amount of psychological research tells us that buying an experience will reportedly make you happier than buying a material possession.[19] That's because everything about the experience—the anticipation, the event, and the memory of or nostalgia for the event—is more powerful than the corresponding feelings when buying a material item.[20]

## ✈ GETTING OLDER & WISER

Would you believe that happiness increases with age and peaks while we are in our 70s? Several studies, including a 2011 Gallup survey of more than 500,000 Americans, have found that emotional health peaks around age 75.[21] More recently, researchers from Dartmouth College and the Wharton School at the University of Pennsylvania found that many older people were happier with their daily experiences than those who were age 18.[22]

# AM I READY TO RETIRE?

Because financial preparation for retirement is so crucial, we sometimes forget that it's just as important to prepare yourself emotionally and psychologically for this new chapter in your life. Being ready for retirement does not just happen once you reach a certain age. This quiz will help you get a sense of where you stand today in terms of retirement readiness.[23]

| | | | |
|---|---|---|---|
| 1. | I enjoy my 9-to-5 job. | Yes | No |
| 2. | My work inspires me. | Yes | No |
| 3. | If money weren't a factor, I would still work. | Yes | No |
| 4. | My social life is closely linked to my work. | Yes | No |
| 5. | I can't imagine doing anything else. | Yes | No |
| 6. | I have hobbies and interests outside of work. | Yes | No |
| 7. | I would stay busy even if I didn't have a job. | Yes | No |
| 8. | I'd enjoy spending more time with friends and family. | Yes | No |
| 9. | I would like to volunteer and help others. | Yes | No |
| 10. | If my spouse retired too, we'd enjoy more time together. | Yes | No |

➜ If you answered mostly "No" to statements 1 through 5, and mostly "Yes" to statements 6 through 10, it's a good indication that you are ready for something new and are emotionally prepared to retire.

# The Ben Franklin

I was having a discussion recently with my mother-in-law. I told her I was trying to work through a tough personal decision and I couldn't make up my mind.

"Why don't you do a Ben Franklin?" she asked.

"What's a Ben Franklin?" I replied.

"You know, you draw two columns, one for pros, the other for cons."

I'd made many a "Ben Franklin" without ever having called it that. I'd always called it a pros and cons list, but I was intrigued to learn this nickname and wanted to know more about it. It turns out that Franklin, the founding father, famous inventor, and leading thinker of his time, is credited with the first two-column comparative decision list. He described the rationale in one of his correspondences:

> My way is to divide half a sheet of paper by a line into two columns; writing over the one Pro and over the other Con. Then during three or four days' consideration, I put down under the different heads short hints of the different motives, that at different times occur to me, for or against the measure. When I have thus got them altogether in one view, I endeavor to estimate their respective weights; and where I find two, one on each side, that seem equal, I strike them both out. If I judge some two reasons con equal to some three reasons pro, I strike out five; and thus proceeding, I find where the balance lies; and if after a day or two of further consideration, nothing new that is of importance occurs on either side, I come to a determination accordingly. —*Benjamin Franklin*[24]

What I love about this description is that he's talking about more than the simple pros and cons list that I had imagined. What Franklin describes is a thoughtful chart of grappling with a decision over a period of days. He considers his own biases and motives, reorganizes and crosses out items, reweighs. Using lists and diagrams and doodles can be a very powerful way of sparking creative decision making.

> Work as long as you find your job interesting. Have lots of friends and lots of interests. Take time to read and enjoy nature. Always set aside time for yourself, to relax, enjoy your health, and your friends. Stay away from any activities or people that are negative. Love life. It is too short.
>
> LOU, RETIRED IN WINNETKA, CALIFORNIA

## Deconstructing Your Life

One exercise that reminded me very much of what Ben Franklin was getting at is something that designer Ayse Birsel describes in her wonderful book, *Design the Life You Love*.[25] It's a glorified doodling exercise, but it can yield fun and sometimes extremely enlightening results. Birsel calls it a deconstruction, a way of breaking something up into its elements to get a fuller picture—and perhaps a deeper understanding.

The exercise starts with a single word (within a circle or square if it helps), which you then break down into parts. Those parts can be broken down into parts, and so on.

I love this exercise for honing in on what's most important in your life. If you started with the words "My Life" in the center, it might look something like this:

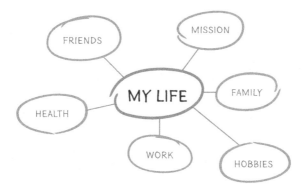

Or you could start with something very specific in the center. Here's
my deconstruction of the word *retirement*:

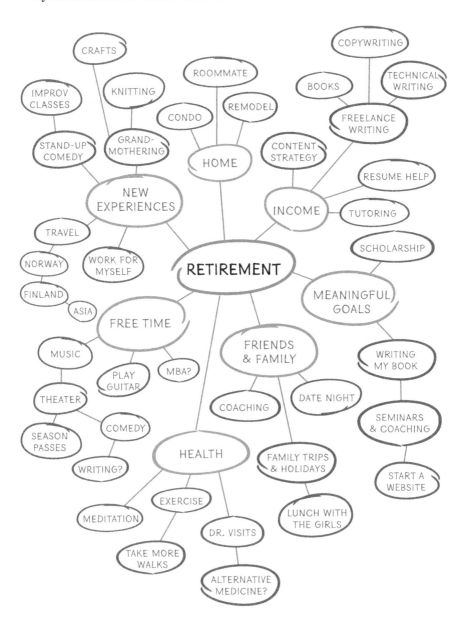

## WORKSHEET 1.1 **DECONSTRUCT YOUR LIFE IN RETIREMENT**

Now it's your turn. Using the chart below, deconstruct the word *retirement* or the word *life* to get a sense of what is most important to you. You can do this right in the book or take out a large, clean sheet of paper. Create your own rudimentary chart. Don't be shy; let your imagination run wild.

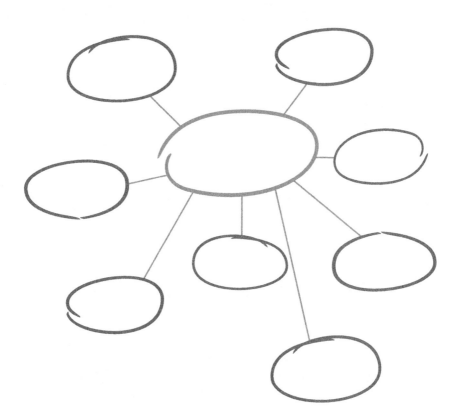

# The 10 Things That Are Most Important to You

This is the type of exercise that seems easy to do until you actually take the time to do it. Can you pinpoint the 10 things that are most important to you?

Personally I find this exercise challenging. What are the things that matter most to me? Writing would be near the top. Also, spending time with friends and family. I love music, as a listener and a barely passable guitar player. I love theater, concerts, and movies. Humor and comedy are important to me; I love to laugh. I care about improving my community, which means I often volunteer my time. I have grown to enjoy regular exercise, especially bike riding. I love to travel and experience new things, especially new foods. If I had all the time in the world, I'd love to spend it painting or making costumes. If I were to organize my life around a mission, I'd love to help everyone I know get a basic understanding of money.

## WORKSHEET 1.2 **10 IMPORTANT QUESTIONS**

To help you think about what is most important to you, I came up with 10 questions designed to push your emotional buttons.

1. My favorite ways to spend time include

2. My least favorite ways to spend time include

3. My favorite people to spend time with include

4. If I could turn a hobby into a business, I would

5. If I could do something just for fun, I would

6. If I could work anywhere, I would be

7. Something that sounds like fun but isn't fun to me is

8. I've always wanted to

9. I sometimes regret that I never

10. If I could give one thing to the world, it would be

## WORKSHEET 1.3 **WHAT MATTERS MOST?**

Take a look at your answers to the previous questions. What stands out?
Transfer 10 of those things to this list.

1.

2.

3.

4.

5.

6.

7.

8.

9.

10.

→ Congratulations! Now you know what matters most to you.

Keep track of this list, because we will come back to it later. You will definitely
need it in your post-retirement life.

# The Scary Stuff

For many of us, happiness simply means the opposite of misery. If we're not miserable, then that amounts to being happy . . . or at least happy enough.

Now that you've focused on the things you love and value, let's switch gears and start thinking about what you fear most. Think of this as contingency planning. You're facing all of the fears that are holding you back so you can factor them into your retirement plan.

## WORKSHEET 1.4 **WHAT SCARES YOU?**

In no particular order, list the 20 things that are most likely to cause you fear, anxiety, or dread.

1.

2.

3.

4.

5.

6.

7.

8.

9.

10.

11.

12.

13.

14.

15.

16.

17.

18.

19.

20.

➜ Now cross out any that are not likely to actually happen (like falling into a pit of highly intelligent rats, one of my personal fears). Examine your list and carve out the top five fears or worries that might actually become an issue during retirement.

1.

2.

3.

4.

5.

➜ This is another list you'll want to keep handy. By the time you reach the end of this book, you will have anticipated, addressed, and hopefully abolished these fears.

## WORKSHEET 1.5 **YOUR WORST-CASE SCENARIO**

This one is a little crazier, but it works. Imagine you are sleeping peacefully in bed at night. Suddenly, you wake up, startled by a frantic version of yourself—a you from the future. Future you delivers a warning that your retirement plan has failed miserably. Consider this scene and answer the following questions based on your worst fears.

What went wrong?

Why did it happen?

What could you have done to avoid it?

➤ Thank you for your answer. Now that we know what you're afraid of, we can build work-arounds for your worst-case scenarios and strengthen your retirement.[26]

## WORKSHEET 1.6 **BACK TO THE FUTURE**

Go back to imagining yourself sleeping peacefully in your bed. Again, your future self wakes you up. This time, future you shares great news. You are happier than ever, and you're ready to share the secrets of your successful retirement.

What does that retirement look like?

How do you spend your time?

Did you try anything new or surprising?

Who did you spend the most time with?

What makes you happy?

➤ I hope the worksheets in this chapter helped you understand what you want to prioritize in retirement and the fears you can let go of. Some of your answers will play a role in your retirement and some of them may translate into new income opportunities. Not all of the things that make you happy will actually make you money, but you may see a pattern developing that leads you toward your dream job. You may even have an epiphany that points you exactly where you need to go.

# GET IT DONE

## HAVE YOU . . .

- ☐ Determined whether you are emotionally ready for retirement?
- ☐ Deconstructed your life and your retirement by drawing a cluster of associated words?
- ☐ Written down the 10 things that matter most to you?
- ☐ Used "what if" scenarios to get a sense of the fear or anxiety that's holding you back?
- ☐ Clearly pictured your ideal retirement?

## RESOURCES

Encore.org. This nonprofit supports a growing movement of older people who are shifting away from their initial careers and using their passions, skills, and experience to make a difference in the world. You'll find inspirational stories of the people who have won the organization's Purpose Prize, which has been called the MacArthur genius grant for retirees.

*Happiness: A Guide to Developing Life's Most Important Skill*, by Matthieu Ricard and Jesse Browner. This is my favorite read on happiness so far. This book covers the topic from every angle and is endlessly fascinating.

*Stumbling on Happiness* by Daniel Gilbert. This smart, entertaining book, written by a Harvard psychology professor, presents surprising connections between happiness and how we think about the future.

Ted Playlists: What makes you happy? (www.ted.com/playlists/4/what_makes_you _happy). This list of videos includes thirteen of the best discussions of happiness to come out of the TED Talks series. Daniel Gilbert is included, along with behavioral economist Daniel Kahneman, writer Malcolm Gladwell, and playwright Eve Ensler.

Zen Habits.net. A father of six learns to simplify his life and becomes happy, healthy, and wealthy. His posts and programs help you develop your own mindful "zen habits."

Action for Happiness 10-Week Online Course (www.actionforhappiness.org/the-action-for-happiness-course). Endorsed by the Dalai Lama, this practical course offers an extensive look at peace of mind, harmonious relationships, improving work life, making the world a better place, and more.

# TWO

# Understand Your Savings

It's time to get a handle on your finances. You knew this was coming, right? Even the easiest retirement plan is going to require a frank look at your assets.

This is the first of three chapters that will help you figure out how to effectively tap your savings, estimate your expenses, and create a budget you can live with. If your finances are already in order, these chapters will be a fairly painless refresher. If not, be prepared to do some work.

Most retirement guides start with expenses, because they are fairly easy to estimate and to adjust as necessary. We will get to expenses next, in chapter 3, but I like to tackle savings first because it's difficult. It may be painful, and taking a close look may be a little ugly, but remember, everything gets easier from here.

Our goal is to get a realistic picture of where your finances are today so we can create a retirement plan that works for you. Even if you aren't planning to retire for another five to ten years, this is a step that needs to happen. You may realize that you are in better fiscal shape than you thought or that you need a plan that involves more working and saving. But it's important to embrace reality rather than live in fear.

In this chapter I'll give you practical information, easy-to-use worksheets, and other resources to help you roughly estimate your predictable income from Social Security, pension, and annuities, and your investment income from 401(k)s, IRAs, and taxable investment portfolios. We'll also talk about some investing strategies for the money that remains in the portfolio throughout your retirement, because your savings need to continue working after you retire. I've included several withdrawal strategies later in the chapter, to show you how to pull money from your investments while keeping the portfolio intact.

## Number Envy

People talk a lot about net worth. Warren Buffett's net worth is somewhere around $60 billion, depending on the day. Oprah Winfrey, with a net worth of around $3 billion, is still only number 603 in *Forbes* magazine's annual ranking of richest people. Rapper Jay-Z is reportedly worth a little over half a billion, which is double Judge Judy's $250 million estimated net worth.[27] In the world of gossip, net worth is a handy stat. But don't be too impressed with the net worth of others or too discouraged by your own.

Net worth is simply the amount of money you have today minus any liabilities, like debt or mortgages. Figuring out your net worth would look something like this:

| Everything I own | – | Everything I owe | = | Net worth |
|---|---|---|---|---|
| *(House, vacation property, cars, stocks and bonds, retirement accounts, hard assets, art and collectibles)* | | *(Mortgage, student loans, taxes, credit card debt, car loan)* | | |

To me, this number feels about as important as an SAT or IQ score. Sure, a bigger number is better, but it's what you do with what you have that counts. If you make far more than you spend or simply make wise investments, you could amass a substantial net worth at any income level. On the other hand, the wealthiest and highest-paid people can spend more than they make (or, more often, forget to pay their income taxes) and could have a lower net worth than you.

## Net Worth vs. Net Income

When you are retiring, you want your net worth to generate safe, steady, tax-efficient paychecks. Instead of clumsily taking out as much as you need each year, you want to create a withdrawal plan that makes your portfolio last as long as possible. If the plan falls short of your needs during the early years of retirement, we can make up for it in other areas (cutting expenses, saving more, bringing in extra income from work). But you must first define the gap in order to bridge it.

There are a few steps involved in drawing down your savings: calculate how much you have in total, decide how much of those savings to draw from each year, and determine how to allocate the assets that remain invested. This is true for your taxable investment portfolios as well as your tax-favored retirement accounts, but the type of account you are pulling from can help you determine the order in which to take withdrawals. We'll discuss this later in this chapter.

I recommend that you get comfortable with the idea of taking some investment risk. Even after you retire, your savings need to grow. Retirees are often advised to move money into the relative safety of bonds and cash. While it's true that a portion of your portfolio should be allocated to fixed-income and cash-like investments, it is wise to balance these with some stock mutual funds. I know, any stock investor who lived through the tech bubble of 2000 or the Great Recession of 2008 knows the risk that comes from equity investing can be painful. But if you want to build net worth and net income, equities can provide the growth. Over the long term, equities provide regular growth of about 10 percent per year on average. Plus, in the age of low interest rates that we live in, bonds don't provide the type of income that can sustain a portfolio or a lifestyle. If you worry about risk, consider the inflation risk that bonds pose, which can do as much damage to your long-term portfolio as stock volatility.

It's all about finding a balance—between growth and safety, stocks and bonds—following smart investing guidelines, and keeping short-term cash on hand. The old trick of investing your age in bonds and the difference between your age and 100 in stocks may make sense if you want 60 percent of your money in bonds at age 60. On the other hand, a 50/50 or 60/40 stock/bond mix may make more sense, but it truly depends on you as an investor. Warren Buffett, widely considered the greatest investor, is said to have recommended that "the average person, who is not an expert on stocks" should invest 90 percent of assets in a low-cost Standard & Poor's 500 Index fund and the other 10 percent in short-term government bonds.[28] Your asset mix should fit you.

## WORKSHEET 2.1 **CAN I AFFORD TO RETIRE?**

The quickest way to calculate whether you can afford to retire is to estimate your expenses in the first year of retirement, then subtract predictable income such as Social Security, pension, or annuities. This will define the gap, giving you the amount of additional income you need to generate each year.

| $ _____ | − | $ _____ | = | $ _____ |
|---|---|---|---|---|
| Year one expenses | | Predictable income | | Amount you need to generate in income |

Let's assume you want your portfolio to last at least 30 years, in which case you'll need about 25 times the annual income amount in your investment portfolio.

$ _____ × 25      =      $ _____

Annual income needs

➤ If your current investment portfolio will already meet your needs, congratulations, you are ready to retire. For most of the people I know, this number will serve instead as a starting point. Now we'll start adjusting some levers to bring your needs in line with reality.

# Predictable Income

Income in retirement can be broken down in many ways, but we're going to start with two categories: predictable (or guaranteed) income and investment income.

To figure out how much money you'll have in retirement, it helps to start with the income you know you can count on. Predictable (or guaranteed) income includes Social Security, defined benefit pension plans, and any guaranteed annuity streams that you receive. Because these are income streams you can count on, in good times and bad, they will be the building blocks of your retirement plan.

## WHAT CAN YOU EXPECT FROM SOCIAL SECURITY?

Social Security retirement benefits represent about 38 percent of monthly income for the average retiree. It may represent more or less for you, but the best thing about it is the guarantee. Once you start collecting benefits, you can count on them for life. They even adjust with inflation, according to the Social Security Administration's (SSA) annual cost of living adjustment (COLA).

Before you file your claim, it helps to get a sense of how much you might be getting each month. Timing counts in this decision. Waiting until age 70 to claim your Social Security will result in the biggest monthly benefits check. If you plan to start receiving benefits before then, you need to understand how the Social Security program works in order to make the most of it.

## WHO QUALIFIES FOR SOCIAL SECURITY?

To qualify for Social Security retirement benefits, you must have worked and paid into the system through payroll and self-employment taxes. If you've ever looked at a paycheck and wondered who FICA is and why you're giving it so much money, you've paid into Social Security. If you didn't work, but you are or were married to someone who did, you may be entitled to receive some spousal Social Security benefits, which can be as much as 50 percent of what your spouse collects after full retirement age. If you have your own benefits in addition to spousal benefits, you are entitled to your own. But if spousal benefits are higher, you'll get a combination of the two.

If you are divorced but were married for at least 10 years and haven't remarried, you may collect spousal benefits on your ex-spouse's record, under similar guidelines. Widows and widowers may get lifetime Social Security survivor benefits, which will be about the same as Social Security benefits. If you take them before full retirement age, the amount you receive will be smaller because you will be receiving benefits over a longer period of time.[29]

## WHEN CAN YOU RECEIVE SOCIAL SECURITY?

You can begin receiving Social Security benefits anytime between age 62 and age 70, but you will receive a reduced monthly income if you start taking benefits before full retirement age. Full or normal retirement age is between 65 and 67 depending on the year you were born.

TABLE 2 **"NORMAL" RETIREMENT AGE FOR SOCIAL SECURITY**

| YEAR BORN* | FULL RETIREMENT AGE |
| --- | --- |
| 1937 or earlier | 65 |
| 1943–1954 | 66 |
| 1960 or later | 67 |

Source: SSA.gov

*If you were born in between these years, your full retirement age is between the two ages. For example, for those born in 1959, full retirement age is 66 and 10 months.

If you wait to claim benefits after full retirement age, you can receive something known as delayed retirement credits, which will increase your monthly income for each year you wait to collect.

Anyone who wants to retire should do the analysis. You might even find out you can retire when you originally thought it was not possible.

MICHELE, RETIRED IN WINNETKA, CALIFORNIA

## HOW MUCH DOES SOCIAL SECURITY PAY?

The average retirement income benefit from Social Security in 2015 was $1,328 per month. The maximum monthly benefit was around $2,663. What you get will depend on a number of factors, including how much you've earned during your 35 highest-paid working years, as well as when you start collecting benefits. If you start collecting at age 62, you will receive 25 percent less in monthly benefits than you will receive at full retirement age. On the other hand, if you wait until age 70 to collect, delayed benefit credits can increase your benefits by as much as 32 percent.

Another factor is marriage. If you are married, you are entitled to up to 50 percent as much as your spouse receives at full retirement age. If your own work record entitles you to more, you get whichever amount is greater.

Widows continue to receive 100 percent of the lifetime income of the deceased spouse. That's another reason it's important to consider any options that boost your monthly benefits, because they will turn into survivorship benefits for your spouse.

## WORKSHEET 2.2 **YOUR SOCIAL SECURITY BENEFITS**

The SSA sends out your "Social Security Statement" once every five years after age 25. It shows you what you can expect to receive in future benefits, and it gets more accurate as you near retirement age and your income history begins to stay fairly predictable.

If you sign up for an online account with the SSA's excellent website at ssa.gov/myaccount, you can access this information whenever you want. I encourage you to do that now, and keep track of your results by writing them here.

Social Security monthly benefit at full retirement age:

$ _____ × 12 = $ _____ per year

Social Security monthly benefit at current age (if applicable):

$ _____ × 12 = $ _____ per year

Social Security monthly benefit at age 70:

$ _____ × 12 = $ _____ per year

Spousal monthly benefit at spouse's full retirement age:

$ _____ × 12 = $ _____ per year

➤ The SSA website is also a great resource for all sorts of tools and calculators that can help you estimate your benefits. For a quick calculation, all you need is your date of birth, earnings in the current year, and the date you've decided to retire. You can even see benefits in today's dollars or inflated future dollars. Similar calculators can let you determine spousal benefits, the impact of retiring early or late, and more. Visit ssa.gov/planners/benefitcalculators.htm.

## WHAT CAN YOU EXPECT FROM YOUR PENSION?

If you are among the fortunate few—currently less than one-fifth of the US private sector workforce—entitled to a traditional pension[30] or defined benefit plan, you have guaranteed income coming to you.

There are a lot of things to like about a defined benefit plan. It's a retirement plan in which employers pay for the retirements of their workers. With a defined benefit plan, the employer guarantees a set income in retirement based on the employee's salary and time served on the job. If you have a defined benefit pension, you could receive monthly income that represents much or all of the income you earned while you were working. Even if it's nowhere close to your working salary, any fixed income helps. You may even have a provision to keep paying pension income to your spouse after you die.

And you should be able to count on it. The federal government oversees pension plans and protects promised benefits through something called the Employee Retirement Income Security Act (ERISA). If your company fails before you retire, you may also be protected by the federal Pension Benefit Guaranty Corporation (PBGC), which protects pensioners in corporate bankruptcy. However, if your company fails, you may not get exactly the amount you were promised. And the PBGC covers only private employee pensions. With government pensions facing underfunding, and few jurisdictions looking to raise taxes, pensions guarantees may shift over time. (Don't panic. According to recent statistics, state and local pensions seem to be generally healthy and earning a good rate of investment return.[31])

Your employer may also offer another type of plan that sounds similar but works quite differently: the defined contribution plan. Defined contribution plans, which include 401(k) and 403(b) plans, are retirement accounts in which you, the employee, are responsible for saving and investing a portion of your own salary. Your employer might chip in with a matching contribution made to your account based on how much you saved. (If you are entitled to an employer match in your retirement plan, save at least as much as that amount. Anything less is like saying, "No, thank you," to your own money.)

If you have access to defined contribution plans, I encourage you to contribute the maximum allowable amount to them, especially in the years leading up to your retirement. Investing in a tax-deferred vehicle like a 401(k) or 403(b) can help your savings compound more quickly, and the contributions are removed from your taxable income, which lowers your total tax bill.

## 5 QUESTIONS TO ASK ABOUT YOUR PENSION

1. **How much will I get?**

   If you are offered a defined benefit plan through work, your employer will have a standard means of calculating how much each employee receives, based on salary and tenure. You can simply ask your human resources representative or the company that runs your plan for an Individual Benefit Statement, which will give you a snapshot of where your benefits stand today and how they could accrue over time. If your plan administrator offers online resources, they may include an interactive calculator or worksheet specific to your benefits and your company's vesting schedule. Vesting is the rate at which you receive full benefits over time. See page 49 [Two Types of Vesting] for more on vesting.

   Individual Benefit Statements must be sent to employees every three years, so you might already have a recent copy lying around.

   If you worked for companies in the past that may have offered defined benefit pension plans, contact them for an Individual Benefit Statement as well. You never know what could be coming to you, so investigate as thoroughly as you can.

2. **When can I start receiving pension benefits?**

Typically, you can't access pension benefits before age 65 or 67. However, you may be entitled to receive early retirement benefits as early as age 50 or 55, depending on your company and your plan. As with Social Security benefits, the longer you wait to receive payments, the higher the payments will be.

3. **Will I get a monthly fixed payment or a lump sum?**

You will probably have a choice between receiving your benefits as a monthly annuity for life or getting the money at once in a lump sum. It's easiest to opt for the steady monthly income, which you can build a budget around, and probably the better option if you need the income to pay your regular expenses. If you take the lump sum, you will be in control of how it's invested and spent, but you risk losing money if your investment goes south.

If your company offers a cash-balance plan, you have the ability to take a lump sum if you leave the company before retirement age. That money can be moved into a rollover IRA and reinvested.

4. **Will the fixed payment adjust with inflation over time?**

If you are offered a fixed payment, the value of that money may be reduced by inflation over time. Some pensions do offer COLAs, typically in years when the plan is overfunded, or taking in more than it pays out. Otherwise, you may be out of luck. The plan administrator will likely let you know about COLAs before they happen.

5. **Will I pay taxes on my pension income?**

Your pension income is taxed at regular income rates, so expect something equivalent to the taxes you paid while working. If you are making less now, your income tax rate should be lower. And you may get a break on state taxes depending on where you live.

## WORKSHEET 2.3 **CALCULATING PENSION INCOME**

Now let's figure out your pension income.

---

$ _____ × 1.2% × _____ = $ _____

Average salary of
my top five earning
years with the
company

total years
with the
company

annual benefit

*(e.g., $80,000 × 1.2% = $896) ($896 × 30 = $26,880)*

---

Monthly benefit:

$ _____ annually ÷ 12 = $ _____ per month

---

Taxes:

$ _____ annually ÷ 12 = $ _____ per month

---

Spousal death benefit:

_____ % of employee's    or    $ _____
benefit will go to spouse          in annual benefits

---

Monthly benefit:

$ _____ annually ÷ 12 = $ _____ per month

---

## TWO TYPES OF VESTING

Vesting is the rate at which you receive your pension, stock options, or employer match benefits. Vesting schedules vary, but they may take five, seven, or ten years. Once you are "fully vested," you are entitled to 100 percent of the benefit.

The two types of vesting schedules are called graded vesting and cliff vesting. Or, as I like to think of them, stepping and leaping.

1. **Graded vesting**

   Graded vesting happens gradually, with the employee earnings typically stepping up an additional one-quarter or one-fifth of the full benefit each year, to reach full vesting at year five or seven.

2. **Cliff vesting**

   With cliff vesting, you accrue benefits but can't touch them for a set period of time, say five years. If you stay that long, you get them all at once.

# Investment Income

The income you earn from your investments can vary for many different reasons. It can rise and fall with the market, and you can decide on how much and how often to draw from it. Where you have your money saved and the order in which you withdraw funds from different types of accounts will make a difference in your strategy. It's all up to you. No pressure, right? But if you have a good plan, you can sustain your investments—and the income you can draw from it—for decades.

## TACKLE TAXABLE INVESTMENTS FIRST

When you start drawing money from your investment accounts, experts typically recommend spending from taxable accounts first, before tapping into tax-deferred accounts like IRAs and 401(k)s, and tax-free accounts like Roth IRAs and Roth 401(k)s.

One of the benefits of selling taxable investments is that you'll pay less tax on them than you will on tax-deferred investments. If you've owned the investment for longer than a year, you will pay only capital gains tax rates on taxable portfolio investment gains—currently around 15 percent for most investors, compared to the conceivably higher rates you will pay on 401(k) and IRA earnings, which follow your ordinary tax rate. Plus, any investments sold at a loss can be used to offset tax on another investment or on ordinary income.

Dividends from taxable accounts are also taxed at a relatively low 15 percent. This makes dividend-paying investments an attractive income option for your retirement plan. Or if you hold hard assets that pay interest or dividend income, such as real estate, drawing that income from this source first is an easy option. Otherwise, a portfolio rebalancing strategy can help you decide what to sell each year. See page 52 [Your Withdrawal Strategy] for more on how to draw down your savings.

WORKSHEET 2.4 **WHAT CAN YOU EXPECT FROM YOUR TAXABLE ACCOUNTS?**

| | |
|---|---|
| Checking account | $ |
| Savings account | $ |
| CD and money markets | $ |
| Investment portfolio | $ |
| Real estate* | $ |
| Alternative assets, collectibles | $ |
| ➔ Total taxable investment assets | $ _____ |

*\* For this exercise, let's consider only investment real estate, not your primary home.*

## WHAT CAN YOU EXPECT FROM
## YOUR RETIREMENT ACCOUNTS?

I'm going to assume you've saved something in your 401(k) or IRA account. If you haven't, spend a year or two stuffing as much of your pre-tax income as you can into retirement investment accounts. If you don't have access to a workplace 401(k) plan, you can open and fund your own IRA plan that basically accomplishes the same goals. The point is, you will need to have savings working for you over the long term, and tax-deferred accounts allow your assets to accumulate more quickly.

This next section will look at ways to draw money out of your tax-deferred retirement accounts. In the preferred order of withdrawal, tax-deferred accounts such as 401(k)s or IRAs come next. Since these retirement accounts are tax-favored, it pays to let them grow over the longest period of time. It's called the magic of compound interest for a reason, folks.

You probably already know that you have to wait until you reach a certain age before taking penalty-free distributions from a 401(k) or IRA. For most people, that age is 59½, but it may be as low as 55 if you were laid off or offered early retirement benefits by your employer. If you withdraw money from retirement accounts before reaching your required age, it'll be costly. You will likely pay a 10 per-cent penalty fee to access your own money, plus significant taxes if you're still in your peak earning years. (The purpose of putting off taxes until retirement is that you will be on a reduced income and pay less in taxes then.) It's also not a good idea to take a 401(k) loan if you are getting ready to retire. If you leave a job, are laid off, or get fired, your loan will become due, most likely within 30 days.

And take note: There's a deadline to start taking distributions from a 401(k), IRA, and Roth 401(k). Beginning at age 70½, you must take a required minimum distribution (RMD) each year or face a penalty.

If you have a tax-free Roth IRA, things are different in a few ways. Contributions that you make to your Roth IRA (and your Roth 401(k)) are not tax deductible, so if you are 59½ and satisfy certain require-ments, withdrawals are tax-free. And with Roth IRAs, there are no RMDs at age 70½ or at any age after that.

# Your Withdrawal Strategy

Beyond the age restrictions, how and when you withdraw your tax-deferred money is completely up to you. But if you want to reduce the risk of running out of money in retirement, it helps to determine a withdrawal plan that provides you with a steady, consistent paycheck over the longest period of time. Below are some of the most well-known strategies. Choose one, or choose a combination of two or more. The important thing is to make your savings last.

## THE FIXED WITHDRAWAL STRATEGY (4% RULE)

One strategy that experts continue to recommend is to set a fixed percentage to withdraw from your portfolio each year. A common rule of thumb is to aim to take 4 percent per year from your investments. This is considered to be at (or near, according to some critics) the rate at which you should be able to safely withdraw income without running out of money.

Now that you know the rule of thumb about drawing 4 percent per year from your retirement accounts, you know more than most Americans. According to a survey from the American College of Financial Services, two-thirds of us have never heard of the "4% rule," and 16 percent of the survey respondents pegged 6 to 8 percent as a safe withdrawal rate.[32]

The "4% rule" presumes that if you withdraw that amount each year from a retirement portfolio invested equally in stocks and bonds, you will be able to sustain your lifestyle for more than 30 years. It comes from a well-known study conducted in 1994 by Bill Bengen, a financial adviser.[33]

The problem with rules of thumb, even thoughtful ones based on thorough research, is that there are many things that could make 4 percent too conservative or too risky. Your life expectancy, the performance of your investments, how much you need to meet expenses, your spouse, Social Security, and whether you continue to earn income are just a handful of the variables that could impact your withdrawal rate. More recently, low interest rates and high stock prices have left some experts questioning whether 4 percent is still sustainable. Other critics say the number is too low. Even Bengen, who has retired after selling his practice in 2013, added more diversification to his strategy and recalculated the safe withdrawal rate at closer to 4.5 percent.

Your exact fixed percentage may be slightly higher or lower, so I recommend you start by withdrawing 4 percent and adjust the percentage as your retirement goes on, depending on inflation and market performance.

Once you have gathered your total investment assets, it's easy to calculate what 4 percent per year would look like.

WORKSHEET 2.5 **4% AND YOUR SAVINGS**

$ _____   ×   4%   =   $ _____

in my retirement savings                in annual income

*(e.g., $1 million in retirement savings × 4% = $40,000 in annual income)*

## THE SYSTEMATIC WITHDRAWAL STRATEGY

A retirement administrator might offer you a systematic withdrawal plan that allows you to dictate the percentage or amount delivered to you each month or year. Using this feature, you could adjust your withdrawal rate each year, starting with 4 percent or so, lowering it during market downturns and increasing it slightly with inflation. The plan is automated, but you can change it at any time to adjust what you take. There is a risk, however, that straying from a fixed plan could cause you to spend your money too soon.

When it comes to investing, the simplest advice really is the best. Whether you choose to do your own investing or hire a professional, here are five tips to keep in mind. For more about working with a professional, see page 59 [Who Needs a Financial Adviser?].

## 1. DIVERSIFY

Investors who are savvy enough to know not to keep everything in a single stock or sector of the stock market sometimes forget that the same goes for holding everything in bonds or cash, which inflation can cause to lose their value over time. Diversification not only reduces risk, it also gives you the chance to make the most of your assets. If one market is up and another is down, you want to hope you are at least invested in both.

## 2. FAVOR LOW-FEE INVESTMENTS

High investment fees can erode your returns, and you need every penny when preparing for life in retirement. Keeping the bulk of your money in passively managed index funds or exchange traded funds (ETFs) will help keep costs low, and for most asset classes the returns are comparable to funds with active managers. (There are great, low-cost actively managed funds that can add value if you're investing in small-capitalization stocks, emerging markets stocks, bonds, and real estate. A bit of research on sites like Morningstar.com can help you find them.

## 3. PAY ATTENTION TO TAXES

How investments are taxed can impact their growth. For example, investing in a tax-deferred 401(k), 403(b), IRA, deferred annuity, or health savings account can increase the compound growth potential of the investment. If you are investing in a taxable account or personal investment portfolio, you have to pay attention to capital gains and losses, mutual fund distributions, and turnover rates. You should consider investments that have fewer tax complications, such as low-cost index funds or ETFs. Another effective tax strategy is to invest today's after-tax dollars for tax-free growth in a Roth IRA. The rules are complicated, but if you hold the account for at least five years, it's possible to withdraw contributions without paying taxes or penalty fees, even before age 59½.

## 4. ADOPT A SIMPLE REBALANCING STRATEGY

I love anything that makes investing easy, and portfolio rebalancing makes it so easy to buy low and sell high. The only decision you make is when you can set aside the time to do it. The emotions and behavioral investing habits that cause so many of us to make the wrong move at the wrong time are off the table with this particular strategy.

Rebalancing means returning your portfolio to its original asset allocation of stocks, bonds, and mutual funds. Rebalancing involves selling anything that's been performing very well to buy more of what has been underperforming. You pick a date to rebalance your portfolio, once a year or every two years, or more regularly if that makes sense for you, and on that date you check your allocation. If no rebalancing is necessary (the allocation is off by less than 5 percent in either direction), you can wait until the next date and check in again.

## 5. AVOID INVESTING IN ANYTHING YOU DON'T UNDERSTAND

As a reporter, I often ask brokers, bankers, investment managers, and marketers to explain something as if I'm a five-year-old. I'd like to think that I'm smarter than the average five-year-old (although I've met some who are pretty sharp), but it has nothing to do with intelligence. What I'm asking for is an explanation in the simplest terms possible, without any jargon or assumptions about what I already know. Money decisions are significant, and you should understand everything about them before writing any checks. Only scam artists will balk when you ask to explain something more clearly or more than once.

## WORKSHEET 2.6 **WHAT CAN YOU EXPECT FROM YOUR 401(K), IRA, OR ROTH IRA?**

This involves looking up your latest statements, but it's worth the effort to get a clear picture of your retirement needs.

| | |
|---|---|
| Total 401(k) or 403(b) assets | $ |
| Rollover IRA assets | $ |
| Total IRA assets | $ |
| Total Roth IRA assets | $ |
| Total Roth 401(k) assets: | $ |
| ➜ Total retirement account assets | $ _____ |

## WORKSHEET 2.7 **YOUR 4% WITHDRAWAL AMOUNT**

Add your Total taxable investments from page 50 to your Total retirement account assets from above to determine your Total assets.

➜ Total assets: $ _____ × 4% = $ _____ per year

## THE BUCKET STRATEGY

The bucket strategy is designed to provide access to cash flow in the short term, while also remaining invested for stability and growth. If you are picturing literal buckets, you get the idea. Each represents a portfolio geared to specific types of investments that you draw from at specific times.

- **Bucket one** In the first bucket goes the money that you need for the next two to five years, or your "safe money." This bucket is kept in cash or cash-like investments (e.g., money market funds, immediate or short-term bonds) that can be drawn from easily and won't be impacted by shifts in the market.

- **Bucket two** The second bucket holds intermediate-term money, which you may need to access in five to ten years. The assets in this bucket would be invested in bonds and balanced funds, and perhaps real estate investment trusts or dividend-paying stocks, which would preserve what you have and could add moderate growth.

- **Bucket three** The third bucket is your riskiest bucket. This is for long-term money that you want to continue to accumulate and grow. A Roth IRA is a great third bucket, because it's designed to be held for the longest period of time. And with the other two buckets offering near-term safety, it's okay to take some investment risks with this one.

Some plans include only two buckets, one for cash and the other for a balanced portfolio. Other plans break the buckets into five-year segments, each invested more aggressively than the next.

## THE ANNUITY INCOME PLAN

I call this the "CYE" plan—cover your essentials. It splits your income types between the essentials and everything else.

Here's how it works. First, you add up all of your guaranteed income through Social Security and a defined benefit pension, if you have one. Next, add up all of your essential expenses, which we will work on in the next chapter. If expenses are greater than income, you can cover the gap with an immediate annuity, which is basically trading-in a portion of your retirement savings for regular monthly payments, guaranteed for life.

Annuities generally get a bad rap in the media because not everyone needs one and they tend to be expensive. I'll put it this way: An immediate annuity could be a great deal if you live 40 more years of volatile markets, because your payments will remain the same throughout. But you may regret the trade if the market skyrockets and your money fails to grow accordingly. And it's a bad idea if you plan to leave assets behind to children or grandchildren. The annuity begins immediately and you're typically locked into it. If you purchase an annuity today and die in a year, the insurance company will claim the money that's left in your annuity. But if you are building a retirement plan around guaranteed income, there aren't many other foolproof sources out there.

With whatever is left in your retirement savings after you buy an immediate annuity, you can invest for growth and choose a withdrawal strategy that covers unexpected or discretionary expenses, including health care, home renovation, vacations, or big-ticket purchases.

## THE REQUIRED MINIMUM DISTRIBUTION STRATEGY

If your tax-deferred retirement assets are still untouched when you reach age 70½, you can decide to take only minimum distributions as a withdrawal strategy. That's the age at which you must take RMDs from a 401(k) or IRA or else you will face a penalty.

You can set up minimum distributions to be automatically deposited into your checking or savings account, so that the annual deadline is not missed. The distributions may vary each year, based on a formula that considers your age and the size of the IRA. Or you can take them according to any formula you choose. While there are many smart ways to take RMDs, if you retire early this is probably not the strategy for you.

In any case, it makes sense to use all the resources provided to help you make withdrawal decisions. Reach out to your plan administrator, your human resources office and/or a professional financial planner to fully discuss your specific options.

Joyce was tired of the daily grind at working in administration at a large health management organization and knew it was time to retire. She didn't quite understand her finances, would usually learn as she went, but it wasn't hard to figure out that if she wanted to retire, she would have to continue to do some work. Doing the calculations, she discovered that she could cut her work hours in half, and by even more than that when she started collecting Social Security in a few years. She talked to her employer about different opportunities, and was able to get work teaching classes in brain health, as well as doing odd jobs like photographing each member of the team for a promotional piece. She has kept herself busy doing fun things she never expected she'd be doing. In the meantime, she paid close attention to her budget, looked hard at big-ticket items, and did not spend money on expensive food, travel, or technology. With a bit of planning, she made it work. "I'm very happy, happier than when I was working," Joyce says. "I feel like my life is moving in a good direction."

# Who Needs a Financial Adviser?

Do you need a professional financial planner or adviser to help with your retirement plan? It's like asking whether I need help remodeling my home. The answer depends on how confident I am about my ability to do the work. A professional planner can help you get a sense of whether your big-picture plan is realistic, but the tools they use will be no different from your own.

Professional advisers offer a variety of services, from a one-time financial plan for a flat rate, to ongoing management of your investment portfolio for an annual fee or percentage of your savings. Some specialize in insurance, money management, or accounting, and large firms may have all of these competencies under one roof. Understand the services you are paying for, so you can determine whether they are what you need.

For example, an adviser can help you set a sustainable portfolio withdrawal rate and strategize your withdrawals to maximize tax efficiency. An adviser may recommend certain investments to balance the risk versus return profile of your portfolio. He or she may recommend an annuity for immediate income.

Friends, family members, and business colleagues can be great sources for leads on trustworthy advisers. Interview a few people before deciding who to work with. Here are a few questions you can ask to gauge an adviser's level of trust and professionalism:

- **What are your professional designations?** There are a lot of designations, so a professional adviser who is serious about his or her career will have at least one. It means they passed a test of knowledge and skill, and are required to stay on top of changes in the profession through continuing education.

  The certified financial planner practitioner, or CFP, is a standard bearer in the profession. A certified financial analyst, or CFA, is another designation that is difficult to earn and shows a level of competency in investment management. Planners with a background in insurance may also have designations such as chartered financial consultant (ChFC) or certified life underwriter (CLU). If an adviser has another designation, ask about what it stands for and what was required to achieve it.

■ **Are you a fiduciary?** Certain investment professionals are held to what is known as a fiduciary standard, meaning they are supposed to put their clients' interests before their own. It's an important distinction, because most fiduciaries disclose any conflicts of interest, take your risk tolerance into account, and make recommendations based on your goals. Nonfiduciaries are held to lesser suitability standards, meaning they are only responsible for putting you into investment strategies they deemed suitable at the time.

■ **How are you paid?** Many brokers and financial planners get paid by investment companies to recommend certain investments to clients. Even if the investment is otherwise good, this type of arrangement might make you question an adviser's intentions. More trustworthy are fee-only advisers, who don't accept commissions and are compensated through an hourly fee, a flat retainer fee, or a fee based on the percentage of the assets they manage. These fees are separate from any expense ratios you will pay for your mutual fund or ETF investments, so make sure you understand exactly what you are paying for the services you receive.

■ **How do you compare to a robo-adviser?** You may not want to ask this when interviewing a prospective adviser, but you should know that there are automated investment advice options. Robo-advisers, as they're often called, are a fast-growing segment of the adviser market. You put your information into a computer program that helps you build a portfolio, then manages the investments over time, at one-third or one-quarter of the price you might pay to get advice from a human. Sites like Wealthfront, Betterment, and Wise Banyan are all established start-ups providing robo-advice, and large investment firms such as Vanguard or Schwab have begun offering automated money management.

# Putting It All Together

There you have it: your income in retirement is likely to come from a combination of guaranteed sources (Social Security, pension, immediate annuity) and variable sources (401(k), IRA, Roth, investment accounts). It's easy to estimate your guaranteed sources of income, and it will be easy to rely on them. But how you invest and withdraw funds from your investment accounts should be carefully considered in an effort to keep your portfolio stable for the next 30 years.

In the next chapter, we'll use the income totals you've gathered here and compare them to your projected expenses. That will give you a better idea of what needs to be done to fill any gaps.

## GET IT DONE

### HAVE YOU . . .

☐ Found your Social Security statement or logged onto SSA.gov to calculate your benefits depending on when you (and your spouse) start collecting?

☐ Estimated pension income, if applicable, via a Pensions Benefit Statement?

☐ Analyzed how different withdrawal strategies might help you access your current or future retirement savings?

☐ Prepared mentally for the idea of taking some investment risk for the sake of long-term growth?

## RESOURCES

"Can I Afford to Retire?" Online Quiz (www.schwab.com/public/schwab/investing/retirement_and_planning/retirement_income/retirement_quiz). From the Charles Schwab website, this is an easy-to-use calculator to get a sense of the big-picture cost of retirement.

Social Security Estimator (www.ssa.gov/retire/estimator.html). Get real-time benefits calculations for yourself and your spouse on this government site. You can also make an appointment or drop in at your local Social Security office and ask someone to walk you through the process. I wouldn't try the phone. Also, try Financial Engines (corp.financialengines.com) for information about Social Security and other retirement planning.

Pension Rights Center (www.pensionrights.org). If you have a pension, and particularly if you're worried about yours, this site covers the news, information, and trends in the world of pension and pension legislation. Phone: 202-296-3776. Address: 1350 Connecticut Ave. NW, Suite 206, Washington, DC 20036.

*The 4% Rule and Safe Withdrawal Rates in Retirement* by Todd Tressider. I've only offered a brief glimpse into the concept of withdrawal strategies. This book (available in a Kindle Edition only) provides an in-depth look, and compares the strengths and weaknesses of a variety of strategies. Tressider's blog, *Financial Mentor* (financialmentor.com) offers general advice about investing for retirement.

Morningstar's "Bucket Approach for Retirement Income" (www.morningstar.com/cover/videocenter.aspx?id=330323). This online video features an interview with superstar wealth manager, Harold Evensky. Evensky invented the bucket approach, and although his strategy is a simplified version with just two buckets, his explanation may help you better understand how it works.

# CHAPTER THREE

# Understand Your Expenses

Remember, back in chapter 2, when I said expenses would be easy? Maybe *relatively* easy would have been a better way to put it. It's easy enough to try to come up with a rough list of what you spend each month, but it takes some time and analysis to get a full picture of monthly, annual, and unpredictable expenses that may arise in retirement. Because the goal of this chapter is to get a realistic sense of what you spend, the worksheets are designed to help you think of every possible expense. And of course you should add other expenses that specifically apply to you.

# How Much Will You Need?

This is one of those questions that make the hairs stand up on the back of my common sense. Because the obvious answer is, "as much as I need today." Indeed, experts recommend that you try to replace anywhere from 80 percent to 100 percent of the income you made while working, because you will likely spend as much or more in retirement.

But bear with me because in the plan I am envisioning you will likely spend less. You will certainly make better spending decisions and allocate your money in a smart way. That starts with thinking of your expenses in terms of needs versus wants.

# Two-Column Thinking

I want to encourage you to get into the habit of putting spending in columns: one for essentials, like shelter, food, transportation; and the other for discretionary items, such as trips, concerts, dinners out, hobbies, and gifts to family. You can customize the columns listed in Worksheet 3.1, but I'd like you to try to extend the categorization to every purchase you make during the next month. If you get into the habit of parsing everything you buy as a need or a want, it can help train your brain to distinguish between the two. I call it two-column thinking, but a better visual might be the little angel and devil that sit on your shoulder when you're pondering a poor choice. Let the needs angel battle the wants devil over every purchase.

To get an accurate sense of your spending in a single month, you can start by looking through your credit card, ATM, and bank statements. A spending journal, where you track every expense down to the penny for a week or a month, will reveal even more details.

## WORKSHEET 3.1 **MONTHLY LIVING EXPENSES**

## ESSENTIAL OR DISCRETIONARY

Separate your essential and discretionary expenses into two columns, with room to move items from one column to the other as necessary.

| ESSENTIAL EXPENSES | DISCRETIONARY EXPENSES |
|---|---|
| Mortgage/rent<br>$ | Dining out<br>$ |
| Water/power<br>$ | Clothing<br>$ |
| Phone/cable/Internet<br>$ | Hobbies<br>$ |
| Home maintenance<br>$ | Entertainment<br>$ |
| Loan/debt servicing<br>$ | Vacations/travel<br>$ |
| Car payment<br>$ | Big-ticket purchases<br>$ |
| Car insurance<br>$ | Charitable contributions<br>$ |
| Public transportation<br>$ | Savings<br>$ |
| Gas<br>$ | Other<br>$ |
| Groceries<br>$ | Other<br>$ |

| ESSENTIAL EXPENSES | DISCRETIONARY EXPENSES |
|---|---|
| Insurance<br>$ | Other<br>$ |
| Prescriptions,<br>medical out of pocket<br>$ | Other<br>$ |
| Misc. (essential clothing,<br>entertainment, holiday gifts)<br>$ | Other<br>$ |
| Income tax<br>$ | Other<br>$ |
| Property tax<br>$ | Other<br>$ |
| Savings<br>$ | Other<br>$ |
| Other<br>$ | Other<br>$ |
| Other<br>$ | Other<br>$ |
| Other<br>$ | Other<br>$ |
| **ESSENTIALS TOTAL** | **DISCRETIONARY TOTAL** |
| $ _____ × 12 months = | $ _____ × 12 months = |
| $ _____ per year | $ _____ per year |

→ Your annual expenses total $ _____

**I** touched on this strategy briefly back in chapter 2, but it bears repeating if you are worried about paying your bills in retirement. This retirement income strategy focuses on making sure essentials are covered by guaranteed income, and everything else can be covered by investment income.

Guaranteed income is anything you know you can count on, including Social Security or a defined benefit pension. It could also include an immediate annuity (or even a variable annuity with a guaranteed income rider), which is an investment that offers a way to turn your savings into regular monthly paychecks.

The balance of your retirement assets, whatever is left after essentials are covered, can be invested for growth. And you can decide on a withdrawal strategy to cover unexpected or discretionary expenses, which might include health costs or inflation.

## WORKSHEET 3.2 **WHAT DO YOU OWE IN CONSUMER DEBT?**

| | |
|---|---|
| Credit cards | $ |
| Auto loans | $ |
| Student loans | $ |
| Cell phone loans | $ |

| | |
|---|---|
| Mortgage principal | $ |
| Mortgage interest | $ |
| Property taxes | $ |
| Property insurance | $ |
| Homeowners/Association fees | $ |
| Maintenance | $ |
| Home equity lines of credit | $ |
| Total home expenses | $ |

# Minimize Mortgage Expenses

Housing is the biggest expense faced by the average retiree. Fortunately, it's one you can anticipate. If you are planning for a retirement that is at least years away, there are things you can do to reduce your costs now and in the future.

■ **Go short** Consider a shorter-term mortgage to reduce the amount of interest you pay over time. A 15-year mortgage can cut costs by 55 percent compared to a 30-year mortgage for the same amount.[34] Depending on the loan, your payments may be the same as they are now, but they will likely be a little bit higher. Still, if you can afford the extra money now, you will be buying yourself peace of mind, and a nice piece of equity, with a shorter-term loan.

I never let my spending for life's needs exceed my pension and Social Security. As far as money from consulting or windfalls, that is spent on fun and on those that I love.

NANCY, RETIRED IN SANTA FE, NEW MEXICO

■ **Go biweekly** This is a favorite trick of mine to help sneak in an extra payment each year. Instead of paying your mortgage monthly, 12 times a year, you can make 26 biweekly payments and effectively make an additional payment. You could also just send an additional payment at the end of the year, but let your bank know you'd like it applied to the principal. This can help you pay off your loan quicker and lower your long-term retirement costs.

## Insurance and Retirement

Just as it's important to plan for regular expenses in retirement, it's crucial to protect yourself from unforeseeable expenses that may come with failing health. Before you retire, consider the types of insurance you may need to protect your savings and ensure a comfortable lifestyle in retirement.

When purchasing any type of insurance, it's important to check on the insurer's financial stability. Independent rating agencies such as Moody's Investor Services, A.M. Best, Fitch, and Standard & Poor's regularly monitor and rate insurance companies. Typically, they are a lot like school grades, with A+ or AAA being the best, but each service will have its own system. If you want a reliable company, it's worth the effort to get to know these ratings, along with your state's department of insurance.

# WHAT TYPE OF COVERAGE DO YOU NEED?

1.  Will you be covered by employer health care until age 65?    **Yes**    **No**

*If you answered "No," then individual health insurance is a must until Medicare kicks in at age 65. Under the Affordable Care Act of 2015, individuals are required to have minimum health insurance coverage or face a fine.*

2.  Will you keep working in your 60s and 70s to fund your retirement?    **Yes**    **No**

*If you answered, "Yes," disability insurance is an important safeguard. If you are faced with long-term illness or injury that keeps you from working, disability insurance can replace a portion of your income.*

3.  Do you have a chronic illness or family health history that may necessitate long-term care in the future?    **Yes**    **No**

*If you answered, "Yes," you may want to look into a long-term care insurance policy. This is insurance that covers care in an assisted-living facility, nursing home, or in-home for extended periods of time. Long-term care insurance can be expensive and complex, especially if you are purchasing it in your 60s; it helps to have a professional advise you.*

4.  Do you want to leave assets to your dependents or provide financial help to loved ones who settle your estate?    **Yes**    **No**

*If you answered, "Yes," then a whole life insurance policy will help. Not every senior needs whole life insurance, but if you have dependents relying on your income or you just want to provide them a safety net, a whole life insurance policy can help.*

Health insurance
premiums                   $ _____ × 12  =  $ _____ annually

   ▪ Out-of-pocket
    expenses              $ _____ × ____ =  $ _____ annually

   ▪ Prescription
    copays                $ _____ × ____ =  $ _____ annually

   ▪ Deductibles         $ _____ × ____ =  $ _____ annually

Life insurance
premiums                   $ _____ × 12  =  $ _____ annually

Disability insurance
premiums                   $ _____ × 12  =  $ _____ annually

➤ Total insurance costs $ _____ annually

# Health Insurance

Your company may cover health benefits in retirement until you reach the Medicare qualifying age of 65. But if you retire early, are laid off, or quit, you may need to find your own health coverage.

Fortunately, it's easier than ever for people to shop for their own coverage through the health insurance marketplace at healthcare.gov. If you are not eligible for or enrolled in another plan through a current or former employer, you may qualify for tax credits that help lower the cost of your annual premium, based on your income and household size. With the new rules in place, you can't be turned down for coverage based on a pre-existing condition.

I have long-term care insurance. I hope I can continue to pay for it monthly and I hope if I ever need it, it will cover what I need.

MADELINE, RETIRED IN SIMI VALLEY, CALIFORNIA

# Long-Term Care Insurance

There are a few things that can derail a retirement plan in which you work less and spend more time doing what you love. One of them is long-term care, or the need for extensive services and support to meet your basic needs for six months or longer. The US Department of Health and Human Services estimates that 70 percent of people turning 65 can expect to use some form of long-term care in their lives.[35]

Medicare only covers long-term care if you require rehab in a nursing home, and it's only for a short period of time (an average of 22 days and a maximum of 100). It also covers some at-home services, again only for the short term. Medicare doesn't pay for daily living assistance, which makes up the majority of long-term care services, according to Medicare.gov. The same goes for most employer-sponsored or private health insurance plans—long-term care services are not covered.

## WHAT IS LONG-TERM CARE INSURANCE?

It's a comprehensive type of insurance designed to pay for personal care services in the home, adult service centers, assisted-living facilities, Alzheimer's special-care facilities, nursing homes, and hospice. Policies typically pay a set amount per day for each type of care (e.g., $100 for assisted living, $75 for in-home care) and will likely limit the amount of money or years spent under that care, so it's important to evaluate individual policies very carefully.

Insurers consider your health and age to determine your eligibility and your premiums. What your policy costs will depend on how

**M**edicare is the large federal health insurance program that covers every American age 65 or older (and, in some cases, younger people with disabilities). If you start receiving Social Security before age 65, you'll be enrolled automatically. Otherwise, you can sign up for Medicare as early as three months before your 65th birthday. If you still have health insurance through work, you can decline coverage until you stop working.

There are four parts to Medicare: Part A covers hospital visits, hospice, nursing home care, and some home health care, but not long-term care. Part B is for doctors' visits, preventive care, and outpatient visits. Parts A and B combined are commonly known as "traditional Medicare."

Everyone qualifies for traditional Medicare via Parts A and B, but it doesn't cover everything. On top of long-term care, benefits that aren't covered include dental, eye exams, hearing aids, and foot issues. That's where Part C and Part D come in. Both can be purchased through private, Medicare-approved insurers. Part C, also known as Medicare Advantage Plans, offers all of the benefits of Parts A and B, plus a little extra, depending on the type of plan you choose. Part D, known as Medicare prescription drug coverage, is designed to supplement what Medicare pays for your medication.

Medicare is not free. There is a premium for Part B, and you will pay a little extra for Parts C or D. There are also deductibles and copays to consider, as well as coverage limits. But because it is government subsidized, premiums are fairly reasonable and predictable. Medicare premiums are deducted directly from Social Security income.

> My long-term insurance is my daughter. I took very good care of her through the years—private school, college, bought her a condo, and gave her a fairy tale wedding. She is now in a position to take care of me so I will let her if it's needed.
>
> DENISE, RETIRED IN WINNETKA, CALIFORNIA

much it pays, the length of your waiting period before the insurance starts to pay, and whether the payments adjust with inflation (they should, otherwise today's dollars may not buy you very much in 20 or 30 years). The average age of long-term care insurance shoppers is around 60, which is probably why these policies have a reputation for being expensive. The policies are cheaper if you buy them while you are relatively young. (In your 50s is still a good time.) Once you face health problems that require long-term care, you no longer qualify for long-term care insurance.

## WHERE DO YOU GET LONG-TERM CARE INSURANCE?

Most plans are individual policies sold by insurers in your state. But you might also have access to a policy through your job. If your employer offers coverage, take advantage of it while you are still working. Workplace policies tend to be easier to qualify for and less expensive. But the coverage must be portable so that you can continue to pay premiums on your own after you leave the job.

Some professional organizations offer group long-term care policies at member rates, but the same portability considerations apply. It may also be possible to find insurers offering joint policies that cover you and another person—a spouse, partner, or family member—as a way to reduce individual costs.

Since long-term care insurance will continue to be an expense in retirement, experts recommend keeping the cost at no more than 5 percent of your retirement income. If your income is very low, you may qualify for Medicaid, which covers some nursing care and in-home services.

Contact the department of insurance in your state to find coverage providers. You can learn whether a given company has received consumer complaints or industry sanctions. And remember to check the credit rating of any insurer to make sure the company is stable.

Before purchasing a policy, get everything in writing and have it looked at by a financial adviser or attorney who is familiar with this type of coverage. Due diligence counts when it comes to long-term care insurance, and you really want to find a policy and insurer you can trust.

# Types of Disability Insurance

Disability policies vary in range of benefits and restrictions. Whether you are searching for the right policy or making sense of the coverage you have, here are some distinctions to know.

- **Short-term disability** coverage provides temporary income benefits for up to six months or a year. Many employers provide this as a baseline of coverage and use it to help offset the cost of extended sick leave or maternity leave.

- **Long-term disability** coverage applies to any disability lasting more than three to six months. Coverage that replaces up to 60 percent of your income can extend for a period of five years or longer.

- **Noncancelable coverage** guarantees you can renew the policy each year without premiums going up or benefits going down. The insurance company can't cancel your policy as long as you keep paying your premium.

- **Guaranteed renewable coverage** can be renewed each year without the policy being changed or cancelled as long as you pay your premium, but the insurance company can raise the annual premium.

Jerry took a phased retirement offer from his large manufacturing company in New Jersey, which allowed him to cut his work schedule to three days per week. Fortunately, he was also able to keep his benefits, including short- and long-term disability insurance. When Jerry broke his leg and couldn't work for three months, disability insurance was there to cover up to 80 percent of his lost income due to missed work. "I was so miserable when I was off my feet," Jerry says. "Disability was about the only good news I had back then." With regular income, Jerry was able to get back on his feet and get his life back in order.

# Taxes and Disability

If you pay the premium for your disability policy, any disability income you receive is tax-free. If your employer pays the premium, your benefits will be taxable.

WORKSHEET 3.5 **5 QUESTIONS TO ASK ABOUT A DISABILITY POLICY**

1. How is the disability defined? Does it mean I can't do my job or I can't work at all?

2. Am I covered for disability arising from illness as well as accidents?

3. What percentage of income does the maximum benefit pay?

4. How do I qualify for the maximum benefit?

5. How long is the waiting period before benefits kick in?

*Source: National Association of Health Underwriters[36]*

**O**ne in four adults will become disabled before reaching age 67, according to the Social Security Administration.[37] If you're relying on income from work at any age, a disability could jeopardize your savings. But as you get older, it becomes increasingly important for workers to protect themselves from the possibility of an injury or illness. That's why disability insurance is a must if your plan is a working retirement.

Disability insurance is designed to replace a portion of your income (typically about 60 percent of the adjusted gross, although policies vary) should you become unable to work. There are government-sponsored disability programs through workers' compensation and Social Security Disability Insurance (SSDI). Employers often include short-term disability and sometimes long-term disability plans among their benefits. And you can also find privately sold, individual disability plans to cover any gaps.

Most people ignore individual coverage, thinking they must be covered under an employer or SSDI. But employer coverage usually only covers the short term, it can be difficult to qualify for federal SSDI, and neither covers everything. If you run your own business or rely on self-employed income, it makes sense to protect it by covering potential loss of income with an individual disability policy.

## WORKSHEET 3.6 **MAKE SAVING AN EXPENSE**

Having sufficient savings remains a priority, even after you have retired. You should aim to have at least four to six months of essentials covered in a short-term checking, savings, or money market account. It helps to make savings automatic, by having money deducted directly from your paycheck into a savings account or investment account. If you need extra help, there's an app called Acorns (www.acorns.com) that will automatically round up to the nearest dollar each purchase you spend on a given card and invest the small amounts for you. It turns savings into a part of everyday life, and you don't even have to think about it.

If you are underfunded for retirement, saving for retirement remains a priority. While you are still working, save at least as much as your employer will match, which may be up to 6 percent of your income, depending on your plan. If you can afford it, take your tax-deferred savings rate to 10 percent of income or even as high as the annual contribution limit (plus any catch-up contributions you might have access to after age 50). If you want to save even more, put after-tax dollars into a Roth IRA for tax-free investment growth.

Savings account contributions:

$ _____ per month × 12  =  $ _____ per year

Annual 401(k) or 403(b) contribution:

_____% of gross income        or        $ _____ per month/year

Roth IRA contribution:        $ _____ per month/year

IRA* contribution:        $ _____ per month/year

Total annual savings expenses:        $ _____ per year

*Traditional, SEP, SIMPLE

➤ Once you've had a chance to think through your expenses, you can use Worksheet 3.7 to make a list that is personal to you. We will need the list, and most important, your total expenses, for work in the next chapter.

| ESSENTIAL EXPENSES | DISCRETIONARY EXPENSES |
|---|---|
| $ | $ |
| $ | $ |
| $ | $ |
| $ | $ |
| $ | $ |
| $ | $ |
| $ | $ |
| $ | $ |
| $ | $ |
| $ | $ |
| $ | $ |

| ESSENTIAL EXPENSES | DISCRETIONARY EXPENSES |
|---|---|
| $ | $ |
| $ | $ |
| $ | $ |
| $ | $ |
| $ | $ |
| $ | $ |
| $ | $ |
| $ | $ |
| $ | $ |

**ESSENTIALS TOTAL**

$ _____ × 12 months =

$ _____ per year

**DISCRETIONARY TOTAL**

$ _____ × 12 months =

$ _____ per year

➤ Your annual expenses total $ _____

# 7 Questions to Ask Your Human Resources Department Before Retirement

1. Will I continue to receive health insurance?
2. What are my health care options?
3. Can I carry over life insurance/long-term care insurance/disability insurance coverage once I leave the company?
4. Will I receive compensation for unused and/or accrued vacation time?
5. What are my 401(k)/retirement plan options?
6. What are my pension benefits? (If applicable.)
7. Do you have any resources to help pre-retirees prepare?

## GET IT DONE

### HAVE YOU ...

☐ Created a two-column list of expenses: needs on one side, wants on the other?

☐ Used the worksheets to include as much detail as you can to make sure you have an accurate view of expenses?

☐ Considered ways to reduce current debt obligations to reduce expenses in the future?

☐ Looked into your insurance options in retirement, including the potential need for disability insurance and long-term care insurance?

☐ Talked to your human resources representative about benefits after you retire?

☐ Calculated your total annual expenses?

## RESOURCES

Medicare.gov. This government site is the place to sign up for Medicare when you're ready. In the meantime, everything you need to know about the Medicare program is easy to find and understand.

AARP's Guide to Understanding Long-Term Care Insurance (www.aarp.org/health /health-insurance/info-06-2012/understanding-long-term-care-insurance.html). One of the most thorough overviews of these complicated policies that I've seen, this guide can help you investigate potential providers and help increase your chances of getting a fair deal.

Consumer Guide to Disability Income Insurance. A document from the National Association of Health Underwriters, which actually has a pretty good site that is designed to simplify the topic of insurance (including disability insurance) for consumers. http://www.nahu.org/consumer/DIInsuranceGuide.cfm

The Bureau of Labor Statistics Inflation Calculator (http://data.bls.gov/cgi-bin /cpicalc.pl). If you want to understand how inflation can reduce your buying power, this simple calculator will show you what the value of the dollar looks like over time.

Getting Rich: From Zero to Hero in One Blog Post (http://www.mrmoneymustache.com /2013/02/22/getting-rich-from-zero-to-hero-in-one-blog-post/). This is a great place to start on a great site, Mr. Money Moustache, written by a couple who retired in their 30s by focusing on happiness and becoming less wasteful.

# CHAPTER FOUR

# Understand Your Budget

Let's just get this calculation out of the way, shall we?

Take your total expected annual income from Worksheet 2.5 in chapter 2, and subtract your total expenses from Worksheet 3.1 in chapter 3.

---

$ _____    –    $ _____    =    $ _____

Total expected      Total projected      plus or minus
income              expenses            income in retirement

---

➜ If the resulting number is positive, you are ready for retirement. But if you haven't planned or saved enough for retirement, this number will likely be negative. That's the gap, and that's okay for now.

If you're underprepared, you will have to reckon with this number at some point. Seeing it in black and white should not put you in a panic; instead, it should give you a realistic goal. Now that you have a number, you can start working toward the retirement you want.

# 3 Ways to Overcome a Retirement Deficit

Short of winning the lottery or receiving an unexpected inheritance, there are three things you can do to bridge an income gap in retirement.

1. **Save more.** Even if you are less than a year away from retirement, now is the time to max out your retirement contributions. If you are older than age 50½, you may qualify for valuable catch-up contributions that let you save even more than the maximum each year.

2. **Earn more.** Continuing to bring in income by working past traditional retirement age reduces the time you need to fund in retirement. We'll get to different ways to create new income streams later in this book.

I budget. I cut down on needless expenses like cable television, home phone service, and daily newspaper delivery.

STEPHANIE, RETIRED IN FT. WORTH, TEXAS

### 3. Reduce spending.

One of the easiest aspects of your financial life to control is spending. Putting yourself on a strict budget can have more of an impact on your savings than you might think. Put that money into a tax-deferred or tax-free retirement account, where even small contributions can grow into something significant.

This chapter is all about reducing your spending. Through careful budgeting, you can find extra money to save and spend. Plus, it's good practice for learning to live on less in retirement.

## Living on a Budget

Remember Worksheet 3.7 in the last chapter? We're going to take that list of essential and discretionary expenses and add a third column, right down the middle.

This space in between your needs and wants is your budget wiggle room. I want you to reconsider your essentials and get a sense of what could be moved to the discretionary column if necessary. You can also hold firm on certain expenses by moving what would be considered discretionary to the essentials column. However, this should happen rarely, so it doesn't merit a fourth column in the worksheet.

# WORKSHEET 4.2 **ESSENTIAL, DISCRETIONARY, AND EVERYTHING IN-BETWEEN**

Add a third column in between your essentials and discretionary. This can also be easily done in Excel if you find the workbook space constricting.

| ESSENTIAL EXPENSES | MOVE? | DISCRETIONARY EXPENSES |
|---|---|---|
| $ | | $ |
| $ | | $ |
| $ | | $ |
| $ | | $ |
| $ | | $ |
| $ | | $ |
| $ | | $ |
| $ | | $ |
| $ | | $ |
| $ | | $ |
| $ | | $ |
| $ | | $ |
| $ | | $ |

**ESSENTIALS TOTAL**

$ _____ × 12 months =

$ _____ per year

**DISCRETIONARY TOTAL**

$ _____ × 12 months =

$ _____ per year

# Mindful Budgeting

Before you move anything from one column to another, I want you to try and imagine a life where you work less, earn just enough, and spend more time doing what you enjoy. Could the freedom of leaving the 9-to-5 world allow you to live more efficiently? Could it be the change you need to cut expenses and stop relying on debt to get by? I'm not talking about commuting costs, pricey office lunches, or work clothes, although you should certainly cut those from your essentials list. I'm talking about a lifestyle change that takes you back to basics.

Imagine being so happy and fulfilled that you weren't driven to spend on the little treats that get you through the day? (Iced quad shots of espresso in giant corporate-label cups are a favorite of mine, as are impromptu weekend stays in nice hotels.) How about the things that are no longer treats, but time-savers that have become an everyday part of your busy lifestyle? (Take-out dinners, drop-off laundry, and those roasted chickens you get at the grocery store are the first things that came to mind.) A recent study found sustained life satisfaction and well-being, as well as improved health among retirees,[38] which might just make all the little extras a lot less necessary.

# 7 Easy Budget Items to Cut

I don't like to tell others how to adjust their budget for the same reason I don't tell them how to raise their kids: it's personal. But I can say with little doubt that we all have room to cut somewhere. Here are a few places where most people have room to reduce expenses:

1. **Groceries/Food.**

   When I was a student, I remember a friend telling me about studying abroad in Asia. I asked her if food was expensive. "I'd buy an apple and a chicken and cook my own dinner for less than $5," she said. It sounded so delicious, and the memory stayed with me for its thrift and simplicity. I always think of my friend's menu when trying to trim my grocery budget. I sometimes challenge myself to make something delicious with five ingredients or fewer, or under $10. Like an economical chef, I have learned to use every bit of food I buy—from the pith and peels to the breadcrumbs and bones.

Not everyone wants to make dinnertime a challenge. But there are other ways to save. Always shop with a list so you don't buy more than you need. Plan meals ahead of time so you are less likely to eat out. Regularly use everything in your refrigerator and pantry; let nothing sit too long. Avoid prepackaged or overly prepared foods. And make good use of leftovers to turn one meal into at least two or three.

If you have the time and interest, there's good money to be saved in coupons. Apps and websites like Coupons, Smartsource, and Redplum make it relatively easy to keep track. Apps including Ibotta, SavingStar, and CartSmart can also help you find great deals and may even give you cash back for purchases if you take a picture of your receipt with your phone.

2. **Cable TV.**

Paying to have a cable company pipe TV into your home is an expense that once seemed essential but now is discretionary, as there are so many ways to watch your favorite shows. Services like Netflix, Hulu Plus, Sling TV, and Amazon Prime all offer ways to access incredible shows for a fraction of the price of cable. Most DVD players and game consoles these days provide the technology to view streaming TV services, or you can purchase a specific module like Roku or Apple TV. If local stations are all you need, a digital antenna may cost you a one-time fee of around $50, enabling you to cut your cable bill completely.

If you aren't sure about switching from cable, start by asking your current provider if there are any discounts it can offer customers who are thinking about cutting service. Major cable providers such as Comcast and AT&T often have special offers for customers who are feeling fleeced.

3. **Car.**

   Going from a two-car family to a one-car family can dramatically cut your expenses for car payments, maintenance, and gas, and it's much easier to do in retirement. If you live in or move to an area with great public transportation or ride-share programs, you could save even more by becoming a no-car family.

   If you decide you really need a car, look for a car with a 10-year warranty or reputation for reliability. The longer you can keep a good car running, the more you will save in the long run. The prevention rule also applies here: regular check-ups and maintenance can save you the cost of major expenses later on.

4. **Insurance.**

   Even if you have great insurance, it helps to shop around every couple of years to see if there are better deals available. If your home and auto policies are currently from different companies, you could save with a bundled policy from one provider. Look into a low-mileage discount on your car insurance after you've stopped commuting, or raise your deductible in an effort to lower your premiums.

5. **Date Night.**

   Remember back in college, when it seemed sophisticated to attend an art opening for the free wine and cheese? Or how exciting it was to stay up all night walking and talking? My point is not to have you question whether the romance has gone out of your relationship, but whether it costs as much to have a good time as you've come to expect. Use your imagination and local culture listings to find no cost or low-cost ways of enjoying leisure time together.

6. **Gym.**

   If you spend a lot of time at the gym, consider it an essential. But there is plenty of exercise to be found without being tied to a gym. You can find free fitness videos on YouTube, look for free local classes at fitness stores, in parks, and community centers. If you're holding onto a gym membership in the hopes that you'll some day feel motivated to use it, cancel the membership and celebrate your freedom with a heart-healthy brisk walk.

7. **Memberships/magazines/recurring payments.**

   Analyze any recurring membership payments that are automatically taken out of your bank account. (Monthly massage and wine clubs, anyone else?) You may realize you're paying for a lot of things without thinking about them. Sure, it seems like only a few dollars here and there, but add them up and those membership clubs are costing you, big time.

# Lighten the Debt Burden

If it feels like an injustice to have to build loan interest into your retirement budget, know that you are not alone. Nearly half of all baby boomers anticipate retiring with debt from mortgage, credit cards, auto loans, and student loans for themselves or a spouse or children.[39] Among American families headed by people age 55 and older, the Employee Benefit Research Institute found that nearly 10 percent had debt payments greater than 40 percent of income.[40]

It's generally not recommended to use precious retirement savings to pay off debt at any point in your career, and certainly not in the years building up to retirement. But if you can take steps to pay off the debt you have without jeopardizing your savings, it will help in the long run. Here are some tips for reducing debt before retirement:

- **Focus on one credit card or loan at a time.** You'll want to first attend to the credit card that charges the highest interest rate. Of course, you're obliged to keep making payments on all revolving debt, but one loan will receive extra attention.

- **Pay more than the minimum due.** For the cards and loans that aren't the focus that month, aim to pay at least $25 to $50 more than the minimum amount due. Paying just the minimum will only keep you in debt.

**C**redit counselors are supposed to help individuals come up with a plan to get out of debt. The services can range from helping you create a budget or debt repayment schedule, to creating a so-called "debt management plan" (DMP) that involves negotiating with creditors, cutting off your access to new credit, and setting up a manageable monthly payment that satisfies your debt.

The Federal Trade Commission recommends avoiding organizations that push a DMP as a first course of action. It also reminds consumers that while most credit counselors bill themselves as nonprofits, they still may be overpriced and may not be reputable. Further, there are steps you can take on your own that would probably work as well as a DMP. But if you are going to use a credit counselor, especially those that solicit by mail or telephone, investigate any potential complaints via Google, Yelp, and your state and local consumer protection agencies.[41]

- **Avoid new debt.** Part of preparing for retirement is getting used to living on less. Start by living on less debt, as in zero. If you do add new debt in retirement, make sure to include it in your annual expenses as it could impact your budget.
- **Consider balance transfers.** If you have good credit and are offered the opportunity to transfer a balance at a 0 percent interest rate for up to 18 months, it may be useful. Be sure to compare the cost of the balance transfer fee (usually located in fine print) to the cost of maintaining the existing debt. Keep the debt separate; don't use the same card for spending as you use for a balance transfer. And make a plan to pay off the debt when the 0 percent interest rate is up, otherwise you may end up owing interest.

- **Try not to jeopardize other savings or home equity.** In the grand scheme of things, your assets are usually more valuable than your debt is harmful. If you come clean to a lender, you may be able to negotiate lower rates or reduced balances if you agree to work with them. There are some cases where even bankruptcy makes more sense than bailing yourself out with desperately needed retirement dollars.

# Reduce Your Housing Costs

In chapter 3, we discussed strategies for paying a mortgage down quickly. Because your home is likely to be your biggest expense in retirement, the lower your mortgage, the more likely you will be able to meet your expenses. But there are other ways to reduce the housing item on your budget.

- **Downsize or relocate.** Simplifying your life in retirement might mean selling the large home in which you raised your family to move to a place that is more modest and has less space to manage, clean, and on which to pay property tax. The balance in equity can go straight into your retirement assets column and could improve your lifestyle in retirement.

- **Get a roommate (or accept the boomerang kid).** If you prefer to keep your big house but don't need all the space, a boarder or roommate brings in extra income. Just make sure to get to know rental laws in your area and make the renter sign a lease with agreed-upon terms. Short-term rentals through companies such as Airbnb are also becoming an appealing option for retirees.

  I've noticed a trend among my friends ever since the 2008 financial meltdown: 30- and 40-something adults are moving back home with their parents. In most cases, rent is involved, making it a mutually beneficial situation for parents and grown-up kids alike. If you have a child or parent who might be amenable to sharing space, it could make sense for you. Make sure that all of the rules, including when payment of rent and expenses is due, is spelled out in a contract that both parties sign.

I was a financial executive and personally like working numbers, so I did a lot of work myself on a financial plan and then validated it with the help of a financial adviser.

JUDY, RETIRED IN PHOENIX, ARIZONA

- **Investigate reverse mortgages.** The key word here is *investigate*. Reverse mortgages are designed to let people age 62 or older turn the equity in the house or condo into monthly cash payments while still living there. Basically, the lender pays you throughout your lifetime and receives the right to keep the property when you and your spouse are gone. That's the pitch, but read the fine print as to how much you get each month, what you pay in upfront fees and closing costs, and who gets the house when. These details make all the difference.

  If you have a lot of equity in your home and no dependents relying on that equity, a reverse mortgage may make sense. Or you may decide a reverse mortgage is not for you. It's the type of decision that should be weighed carefully with a trusted adviser. If you feel pressured to purchase a reverse mortgage, run!

Mary sold her "big" house, the one she had raised her daughter in, at age 54. It was in Providence, Rhode Island, and Mary had been offered a job in New York City. Fortunately, she was able to sell at the top of the housing bubble in 2007. Two years later, she was able to use some of the equity from the house sale to buy a small Brooklyn condo, this time at the bottom of the market after the housing crisis of 2008. She loved the apartment and was happy to see her neighborhood gentrified rapidly. Unfortunately, she lost her job five years later, and decided to move back to Providence. "My Brooklyn condo sold in five days, for $170,000 more than I paid for it three years prior," Mary says. "I bought an adorable condo in Providence, RI, for $78,000. All of my expenses were drastically cut. Real estate has been good to me."

# WHERE SHOULD YOU LIVE?

If you've decided to move somewhere less expensive or just better situated, there are many things to consider. In the end, you may decide to stay right where you are, as Census Bureau data indicates most seniors do.[42] Take this handy quiz to get your wheels turning.

## ☐ RURAL   or   ☐ URBAN

*You probably already know if you have your heart set on retiring in the quiet country or in a bustling metropolis. If you are planning a rural retirement, keep in mind the importance of access to hospitals, health care, groceries, gas stations, handymen, and helpers.*

## ☐ NEARBY   or   ☐ NEW LOCATION

*According to data from the Census Bureau, most seniors stay local, which offers the benefits of a built-in social network and nearby services you are familiar with. But if you are ready for a new location, consider carefully all aspects of your lifestyle that will change. How affordable will your new destination be, in terms of housing costs, cost of living, and taxes? Can you find good doctors and health care services in your new destination? How about things like air quality and crime? Art and education? What is the quality of life?*

## ☐ DOMESTIC   or   ☐ INTERNATIONAL

*If you've ever dreamed of living abroad, the retirement years can be a great time to do it. If you have the flexibility to work from wherever you choose, you may be able to find a beautiful destination where your dollar goes a lot further. The AARP lists some of the best places to retire abroad according to cost of living, access to health care, hospitality toward Americans, and so on.*

*www.aarp.org/home-garden/livable-communities/best_places_to_retire_abroad/*

## ☐ **HOT** *or* ☐ **COLD**

*Retirees traditionally flock to spots that supply year-round heat (Florida, Nevada, Arizona). If you don't mind a cold climate, however, you may have more options. In a recent report from Bankrate, the top states for retirees were midwestern or mountain states like North and South Dakota, Colorado, Utah, and Wyoming.*

## ☐ **WALK** *or* ☐ **DRIVE**

*Is retirement is a good time to give up your car? Walk-friendly retirement spots can help you save money on transportation costs and increase your active lifestyle. Real estate sites like Trulia and Zillow include walkability information, or go to the site WalkScore to find out how your favorite retirement location ranks.*

## ☐ **COLLEGE TOWN** *or* ☐ **QUIET TOWN**

*College towns have garnered attention from the senior set because they are typically vibrant cultural hubs with access to public transportation and good hospitals. Depending on where you look, college towns can also be more affordable than other metro areas. And there are a growing number of university-based retirement communities if you are looking for a senior enclave within a college town. Just be warned that with all that vibrancy comes the occasional all-night keg party that could keep you awake.*

## ☐ **INDEPENDENT LIVING** *or* ☐ **SENIOR COMMUNITY**

*Forget every preconceived notion you have about "old folks' homes"; today's retirement communities are hotbeds for hip seniors looking for fun. Affinity communities let you find a place that caters to people with your interests (sports, art, singles, faith, alumni associations, etc.). Retirement communities typically offer a range of options, from independent living to assisted living, as well as the option to transition from one to the other as you age.*

www.consumerreports.org/cro/2013/07/how-to-choose-an-assisted-living-facility/index.htm

➤ Having a realistic picture of where you stand financially is such an important part of your retirement plan. So while it wasn't easy, you should be proud of yourself for how far you've come. Next we'll try to balance things out by adding just enough income to make your retirement dreams a reality.

## HAVE YOU . . .

- ☐ Calculated your income minus expenses?
- ☐ Determined how to bridge any income gap in retirement?
- ☐ Created a budget and started looking for ways to reduce expenses?
- ☐ Considered whether you want to move in retirement or stay in your home?

## RESOURCES

Consumer.gov Budget Worksheet (www.consumer.gov/content/make-budget-worksheet). This free online budgeting tool can be as sophisticated as you need it to be.

Mint.com. This free online tool and app lets you input all of your financial information and get a clear view of your finances, all in one place. You can use it to budget, track investments, or keep up with credit cards and other bills. Because it syncs with your bank account and credit card transactions, it can crunch the numbers and tell you when your budget is in trouble. As the site learns your preferences and habits, it can recommend financial products that are right for you.

Level Money (levelmoney.com). Another free app, this one simplifies the budget process by giving you a spendable amount for the day, week, or month. You can use it to track purchases and to stop spending once you've reached your limit.

Excel. If you're handy with a spreadsheet, you can easily track your spending in Microsoft Excel or Google Sheets.

Sperling's Best Places (www.bestplaces.net). This site ranks the top retirement cities and allows you to compare retirement destinations according to a variety of factors that may be important to you.

The Milken Institute's Best Cities for Successful Aging report (Successfulaging .milkeninstitute.org). This report was first released in 2012, then updated in 2014. It offers an in-depth look at the more than 350 US metro areas in terms of what they have to offer retirees based on public data for health care, transportation, community engagement, cost of living, and employment and educational opportunities.

ESPlanner (esplanner.com). This financial planning software was developed by a Boston University economist. It integrates all aspects of your financial life to help you set annual spending and portfolio withdrawal targets, and it will even suggest strategies for raising your standard of living. A basic version of the software starts at $149 upfront, plus an annual licensing fee of $50.

*Your Money or Your Life: 9 Steps to Transforming Your Relationship with Money and Achieving Financial Independence* by Vicki Robin. Just the book you need to help you tap into your money values and habits.

Feex.com. This is a cool site designed to help retirees reduce the fees they pay in their retirement plan. You can start for free to see how it works.

# 2

# EARN
# ENOUGH

There's a quaint little town in California's Santa Ynez Valley, just over the hills past Santa Barbara, called Los Olivos. The entire downtown can't be more than half a mile long, and nearly every store-front offers wine tasting for dozens of nearby wineries and vineyards.

I am completely intrigued by the pourers, the people who work behind the counter, pouring and describing the tastings featured that day. They know so much about wine, and particularly about the agriculture and grapes in the area. These are people who seem to truly love their jobs. "When I'm retired . . . " I say aloud every time I'm in Los Olivos.

You might hear me say the same thing in certain cafés in New York's East Village, cool vintage stores in Santa Fe, or in an art museum—anywhere I come across a job I'd love to do if I needed to earn just enough.

It may sound like nonsense—dreaming of the job you'll get to do when and if you have the chance to retire. What about taking more naps, learning to play the piano badly, buying an extra-comfortable beach chair, and finally reading *Moby Dick*? I plan to indulge in all of those things, but I'm also looking forward to spending a portion of my time earning enough at one of those cool jobs that I've been talking about all these years.

An earn-enough job will mean different things to different people. You may need to bring in significant part-time income, create small revenue streams from a variety of sources, or have the financial flexibility to volunteer your time. For some people, the earn-enough job is starting a business or a foundation.

After completing the worksheets in part 1, you should have a sense of how much income you need to bring in each month to bridge the gap between your retirement income and your expenses. The next step is to figure out what your earn-enough job (or jobs) might be.

The good news is that we live during a time when it's easy to find ways to trade on your skills. If you have something you can sell—from business consulting to babysitting—you can find a way to sell it.

In this section, we'll start with evaluating skills and interests, and then figure out a way to market them. We're going to come up with some ways to bring in income and earnings, and then we'll do a bit of a reality check at the end.

## Five Major Milestones

The five steps you will take in this section:

1. Take stock of your skills and interests.

2. Find value in the things you like to do most.

3. Understand the variety and categories of opportunities available to you.

4. Consider the impact that working has on the timing of your Social Security claim and total benefits.

5. Determine what you want to do in your next act.

# CHAPTER
# FIVE

# Your Skills and Interests

There's value locked in your skills and interests.

The things you enjoy doing and do well add value to your life. They are among the keys to happiness that we discussed in chapter 1. But your skills and interests also have monetary value. Enough value that you could create streams of revenue—big or small—to help meet your expenses in retirement.

Whatever it is you do or want to do, there's probably a market out there for it. With today's technology and networking capabilities, there are ways to make money that would not have seemed imaginable decades ago. You can profit from your hobbies, work as a freelancer or consultant using the skills you used in your career, find an interesting or rewarding part-time job, or start a business or charity.

And you're likely to enjoy what you do, as long as you are active and engaged. A study by the Brookings Institute found that late-life workers have higher levels of well-being than retirees who are not working.[43] Flexible retirement approaches also led to greater well-being, according to Brookings.

# The Midlife Career

A series of exciting workforce trends are making it easier than ever for older workers to shift into different types of jobs with flexible schedules and/or the option to phase into retirement gradually. One dramatic trend is demographics. The would-be retiree set represents a portion of the workforce that is growing fast; employees ages 55 and older are projected to make up nearly 38 percent of the workforce by 2022, according to the Bureau of Labor Statistics. This is up from 26 percent in 1992.[44]

In other words, corporate America is growing more and more dependent on people like you. They value your skills and abilities, and are working hard to come up with flexible work schedules, phased retirement, part-time consulting and mentoring, and other options for older workers.

At the same time, there are plenty of possibilities for anyone who wants to create a more flexible work-life through one or more small "gigs." For example, if you've always thought of yourself as a writer, you might look for freelance work in marketing or copywriting. Small and local businesses in particular may be looking for people to help them craft the language on their websites and client communications. You might start a blog to advertise your services, write about a passion, or both.

On the Internet, it seems, there is a lid for every pot. If you are interested in doing something, you can find a way to do it, whether it's tutoring high school students, selling vintage glass, or driving people around town.

Because your options are so vast, it's important to do some self-analysis to figure out what you really want to do. Which skills and interests would you like to market?

# WHAT DO YOU LOVE TO DO?

Read each of the statements below and circle your level of response. Your answers should come easily; after all, one of the nice things about getting to this point in life is that you know your strengths and preferences well.

1. Not true at all; I'm terrible.
2. A little true, but it's not my strong suit.
3. Somewhat true; I'm OK.
4. True, and I'm good.
5. Are you kidding? I'm the best.

---

I am good with my hands—assembly, repair, and mechanics.

1   2   3   4   5

---

I am good with words—writing, speaking, and instruction.

1   2   3   4   5

---

I am good with numbers—accounting, computing, and book keeping.

1   2   3   4   5

---

I am good at analysis and logic—data analysis, data crunching, research, and programming.

1   2   3   4   5

---

I am good with people—helpfulness, motivation, empathy, and intuition.

1   2   3   4   5

---

I am a good manager—leadership, decision-making, and problem solving.

1    2    3    4    5

I am creative and imaginative—design, invention, and engineering.

1    2    3    4    5

I am artistic—music, photography, painting, drawing, and theater.

1    2    3    4    5

## NOW, LIST ANY SKILLS THAT YOU GAVE A 5, 4, OR 3

5

4

3

➤ Does your list help give you a sense of different types of skills you might be able to market? Let's keep working to see if we can get additional ideas.

For some of us, coming up with the dream job is easy, because it's been there all along. It's the career you gave up because you wanted to make real money. It may be coaching, cooking, jewelry making, painting, pet care, social work, teaching, writing, or any number of things that you would love to be paid to do.

That's what happened to Richard, who retired early from his corporate IT job to return to his first love, ceramics. He set up a studio in his basement and was soon spending eight to ten hours a day making mosaic art out of glass and pottery tiles. When he had decorated enough mirrors, flower pots, and trivets, he signed up to exhibit at a local crafts fair. He made enough money at that first crafts fair to cover the expenses for his new-old hobby. When a neighbor visited and saw the gorgeous mosaic mural Richard had made for his kitchen, she commissioned him to create a similar piece for her house. That gave Richard the confidence to think that he could advertise his talents for hire. His son made him a website and posted photos of the mosaics. For the next three years, Richard continued to sell at crafts fairs and was occasionally hired to create mosaic kitchen or bathroom backsplashes and garden walls. Each piece was duly photographed and added to his online portfolio. He began offering mosaic-making classes in his basement studio to ten or twelve students at a time. After completing his class, some of those students wanted to continue making mosaic art but didn't have the space at home, so Richard offered them studio time for a modest hourly fee. Eight years into retirement, Richard's art career is thriving. In addition to an income stream, it provides new social contacts, exercise (lifting all those tiles and bags of cement), and the rewarding feeling that he gets to fulfill the dream he'd once given up.

## WORKSHEET 5.1 **3 THINGS YOU'D DO IF YOU WEREN'T AFRAID TO FAIL**

List three dream jobs or careers that you have always wanted to do. If you have the skills and the motivation, there are any number of ways to make your dream job a reality. The sky is the limit here, because no matter how preposterous you think your answer is, it may help lead you to something that's both attainable and fulfilling.

1.

2.

3.

## WORKSHEET 5.2 **WHAT YOU LOVE TO DO**

Here's another way to help you think about new possibilities for retirement. Starting with the skills you ranked 3–5 in the quiz and the dream jobs you just listed in Worksheet 5.1, create a list of your top skills and interests. Don't feel limited to the ones listed below. They're just to get you started.

### COMMON SKILLS AND INTERESTS

- Collectibles and antiques
- Cooking/baking
- Crafting
- Decorating
- Design and remodeling
- Entertaining
- Fitness/exercise
- Games/strategy
- Gardening
- Health care/nutrition
- Housekeeping
- Investing/stock trading
- Math/numbers
- Nature
- Networking/politics
- Organizing
- Painting
- People
- Pet care/animals
- Reading
- Research
- Sports
- Teaching/mentoring
- Technology
- Travel

## MY SKILLS AND INTERESTS

1.

2.

3.

4.

5.

6.

7.

8.

9.

10.

11.

12.

# Ask Friends and Family

If you really want a good sense of your skills, ask your spouse, friends, and other family members what they think. I know, it sounds like dangerous territory, but if you ask the people in your life to take the exercise seriously for the sake of your retirement happiness, they may just oblige.

One way to get the conversation started is to share the exercises you've completed in this book. Talk about your experience, and the ideas that it has given you.

Friends and family can help support your dreams in more ways than one. As you start looking for a part-time gig in retirement, you're going to want a large network to turn to for potential jobs, contacts, and referrals.

# Assess Your Transferable Skills

You don't need to learn an entire new set of skills to work in a new industry. Certain experience and abilities are valuable to all types of businesses, nonprofit organizations, schools, government agencies, and small startups. They're known as transferable skills, and if you have them, you could conceivably work anywhere. Below is a list of the five most general transferable skills, but each category contains many specific transferable skills. For example, accounting includes the ability to work alone, attention to detail, and math. Analysis includes data manipulation, finance, and problem solving. Organization includes decision making, teamwork, and setting priorities. Communication includes empathy for others, negotiation, public speaking, and writing. Management includes handling responsibility, and social skills. Once you start to make a list, you will undoubtedly find you possess many transferable skills.

Transferable skills include:

- Accounting
- Analysis and interpretation
- Communication
- Management and motivation
- Organization and administration

## WORKSHEET 5.3 **WHAT ARE YOUR TRANSFERABLE SKILLS?**

1.

2.

3.

## EXPLORING NEW SKILLS

If you have a few years to develop a plan for working after retirement, you may have time to pick up some new skills.

One increasingly popular way to gain skills is to go back to school. Students who are older than 35 are soon expected to make up 19 percent of the total undergrads and grad students, according to the National Center for Education Statistics.[45]

Going back to school paid off for Louise, a retiree from Charlottesville, Virginia. Louise spent her career in primary education, first as a biology teacher, then becoming a school psychologist, and retiring as a supervisor of special education classes, where she had served 25 school districts for 10 years. After retirement, she wanted to do something just for her, which turned out to be doctoral school. "I thought I was too old to use it anywhere," she says about receiving a PhD degree. "But when I graduated, the university hired me as an assistant professor to teach teachers of special students for 10 more years. After that I retired for the second time."

If you didn't go to college the first time around, there's no time like the present for higher education. Of course, burdening yourself with student debt at the same time your income will be limited may not at first sound like a wise investment. The good news is there are ways you can learn for free.[46] Here are a few ways to reduce or cut the cost of college.

**TUITION WAIVERS** Large and small colleges and universities across the country offer free courses to senior learners. The Senior Citizen Guide for College lists the waivers for each state (www.aseniorcitizenguideforcollege.com /p/find-your-state-tuition-waivers.html).

**COURSE AUDITING** Most accredited schools have a policy allowing senior students to audit a certain number of classes for free each semester. Contact schools in your area to find out about their course auditing policies.

**TUITION REIMBURSEMENT PROGRAMS** While you are still working, investigate whether your company offers a tuition reimbursement program. Under these programs, the employer reimburses an employee for the cost of his or her tuition and other qualified expenses. While some employers require the coursework to be job-related, others have no restrictions on the courses you can take within their program.

**COMMUNITY COLLEGES** Have a junior college or a community college in your area? These schools are an affordable alternative to pricey universities, and the courses and resources are often similar to those you'd find at a bigger school. One study found that 84 percent of community colleges offer courses for students who are ages 50 and older.[47]

**ONLINE COURSES** There are plenty of ways to get learning for free online. The Kahn Academy can teach you everything from microeconomics to Art of Oceania. There are also a growing number of sites that will teach you how to code computer language. Adding computer coding to your existing skills and experience could make you eminently more hirable.

➤ If you do pay for education, find out whether you qualify for the Lifetime Learning Credit or American Opportunity Tax Credit. These income tax credits can provide a dollar-for-dollar reduction on your income tax bill for a portion of what you pay in tuition and fees.

# WHAT DO YOU ENVISION?

Remember, there's no right or wrong answer to these questions. Some of these may be easy to answer right away, and others may take more time to figure out what it is you want to do.

1. Do you want to work in the same industry or field that you were in throughout your career?

2. Do you want to continue to use specific skills or abilities that you used during your career?

3. Do you want to avoid certain aspects of the work that you did during your career?

4. Are there things you do easily that others can't do as well?

5. Do you need to go back to school or learn new skills for the work you envision?

6. Do you prefer working for a large organization or a small organization? Would you like to work for yourself or do you prefer working for others?

7. Do you feel motivated to change things that frustrate you in the world?

8. Is there a passion or mission that you could envision turning into a career?

9. If you wanted to play it safe, what would you do?

10. If you wanted to take a risk, what would you do?

## ADAPTING AFTER A LAYOFF WITH CONFIDENCE

**I**f you have been forced into an early retirement due to a layoff, you may be dealing with different emotions as you search for a new job. It is not uncommon to struggle with a lack of confidence after a layoff, leaving you in a defensive position during a job search.

I can relate. My small business began after a layoff, and it made the transition filled with doubt. It was particularly bad when I listened to the unsolicited advice from friends and family, because it seemed as if every opinion was designed to add to my own worries and fears.

That's why I recommend the plan outlined here. Confidence is so important and so easily lost due to random chatter, but by thinking through the issues presented in this chapter, completing the worksheets, and doing serious self-analysis, you put yourself in a position of strength. You've evaluated your skills and weaknesses, you know what you want and don't want, and maybe you've even got a few new ideas for ways to translate your skills into income. Combine that with the financial planning work we did in part 1, and you are already on better footing for retirement.

## WORKSHEET 5.4 **WHERE YOU CAN EARN MONEY**

Using the top skills and interests that you've gathered from the worksheets in this chapter, list up to five potential ways to make money for each. Below are some examples to get you started. Some of the potential ways to earn money may seem more comfortable and safe than others. Try to give yourself a mix of what feels safe and what feels risky.

| SKILL/INTEREST | POTENTIAL WAYS TO EARN |
|---|---|
| Communication | Blogging |
| | Copywriting |
| | Public relations |
| | Technical writing |
| Entertaining | Catering |
| | Children's party planning |
| | Event organizing |
| | Wedding/private party planning |
| Innovation | Design |
| | Programming |
| | App building |
| | Website building |
| | Starting a business |
| Mentoring | Coaching |
| | Team leader |
| | Tutoring |

| SKILL/INTEREST | POTENTIAL WAYS TO EARN |
|---|---|
| Networking | Recruiting |
| | Matchmaking |
| | Human resources |
| | Sales |
| | Public relations |
| Organization | Project manager |
| | Personal shopper |
| | Home organization |
| | Executive services to small business |
| | Space planning |
| | Librarian |
| Problem-solving | Office management |
| | Data management |
| | Metrics analytics |
| Social Skills | Social work |
| | Mediation |
| | Elder care |
| | Advocacy |
| | Nonprofit work |
| | Starting a nonprofit |

➤ Try to list five more skills and interests, and for each of those list four potential ways they could earn money for you. Some of these choices may seem more comfortable and safe than others. Give yourself a mix of what feels safe and what feels risky.

| SKILL/INTEREST | POTENTIAL WAYS TO EARN |
|---|---|
| 1. | |
| 2. | |
| 3. | |
| 4. | |
| 5. | |

➤ Congratulations on completing the worksheets in this chapter. By putting these pieces of information together, you are getting a fuller picture of what is possible after you retire. Next up, we'll discuss the different types of work you might pursue in retirement, to find which best fits you.

## HAVE YOU . . .

☐ Evaluated your strengths? If you are feeling stuck, try some different tests online. The Meyers-Briggs is a popular one for hirers. Also, ask your friends and family what they think you are good at.

☐ Started to build a case for the type of job you think you want?

☐ Brainstormed the ways the skills and interests you've listed in your worksheets could potentially become sources of income?

### RESOURCES

*Your Money or Your Life: 9 Steps to Transforming Your Relationship with Money and Achieving Financial Independence* by Vicki Robin.

My Lifestyle Career (www.mylifestylecareer.com/recommended-resources /recommended-sites/100-great-second-act-career-sites/). This is a two-for-one resource. MyLifestyleCareer.com is a great site run by career consultant Nancy Collamer. She publishes a regular newsletter full of job tips and advice for second-act careers. The link above goes straight to the site's list of recommended sites for older job searchers. Collamer's book *Second-Act Careers: 50 Ways to Profit from Your Passions During Semi-Retirement* is also an excellent resource.

KahnAcademy.org. Easy to follow courses can teach you the basics (and beyond) about pretty much any subject you name. It's definitely a good primer if you're interested in learning something new—from marketing a business to learning to code.

A Senior Citizen Guide to College (www.aseniorcitizenguideforcollege.com /p/find-your-state-tuition-waivers.html). It's a long URL (or a quicker Google search) but it's worth the work to access this resource, which lists schools that waive tuition in all 50 states. You can search your state to find tuition waiver programs near you.

Plus 50 Community Colleges (plus50.aacc.nche.edu/colleges/coll_prof/Pages /default.aspx). 100 community colleges take part in the initiative to help boomers learn valuable job skills.

Jobsearch.about.com. This site, run by expert Alison Doyle, has a great deal of useful information and resources you need to find and land a gig. It can help you prepare your resume, find resources that connect you to gigs, and anticipate interview questions.

Skills Profiler at CareerOneStop (www.careerinfonet.org/skills/?frd=true). If you're looking for more potential job matches for your skills, this tool from the US Department of Labor can help you brainstorm.

# Choose Your New Income Streams

Now it's time to apply the skills you've determined are most valuable to potential new income streams. Recall from part 1 that working just enough is one of three options you have to make up an income deficit. The others—save more and reduce spending—could also be part of your plan. You can do a combination of all three. But if you are interested in working, and can work, it is the most effective way to increase the long-term security of your retirement.

As much as I have encouraged you to be creative and bold in thinking about what you might do in retirement, I want you to be realistic as well. The goal is always to bring in enough income to meet or exceed expenses.

Being realistic means, among other things, staying clear of get-rich-quick schemes promising you outrageous returns if you just hand over a lump sum. Retirees are targets for scammers looking to steal an easy buck, so don't give anyone the power to further jeopardize your savings. If it sounds too good to be true, it probably is.

With this plan, the goal is to take the risk out of retiring by making it more realistic and achievable. But we also want you doing something you love; otherwise what's the point in retiring? So even if your plan involves several small income streams over the long term, you can find a way to make your retirement work.

There are as many different ways to earn money after you retire as there are people. But how you bring in income will generally fall into one of the common categories described in this chapter.

# The Scaled-Down Day Job

If you generally enjoy your job but would like to spend less time doing it, you may be able to go part-time. As companies increase their flexible work options, it is becoming more common for retirees to gradually ease out of working life with a phased retirement. An estimated 12 percent of large companies have some type of flexible retirement program,[48] although most are informal plans allowing employees to continue working reduced hours for a few years before full retirement. Formal plans typically allow for tailoring. For example, the federal government introduced a formal Phased Retirement Plan in 2014. To qualify, you need to be in the Civil Service Retirement System or Federal Employees Retirement Plan with 30 years of service and be at least age 55. Under the program you work 20 hours and take the rest in pension, and you must commit to spending time mentoring other employees.

Madeline worked for the same aerospace company throughout her career, until it was purchased by a competitor a few years before she was to retire. Her job would still exist at the new company, but she would have to retire by a certain date to receive her initial company's pension and health care benefits. She continued to love the job under new ownership, and when it came time to retire, the new company offered her a job as a temp, doing the same work she had been doing, but with more flexible hours. This allowed her to collect her pension and keep her health benefits, to push back Social Security claims until age 70, and to continue to save and invest for her nonworking years. Now in her mid-70s, Madeline no longer works, but she

Work as long as you can if you really like your job.

LOUISE, RETIRED IN CHARLOTTESVILLE, VA

volunteers part-time at the reception desk of her local police station, which makes her feel useful and safe.

The impact of phased retirement on benefits is just one thing to consider before taking this type of offer from your company. Find out whether a reduced work schedule impacts any benefits, including pension benefits, health care, disability insurance, and life insurance. Some phased retirement plans also have protections to keep income reductions from impacting these benefits, including Social Security. If yours does not, consider the cost of reduced benefits before making a decision.

# The New Opportunity Job

You know retirement is looming, but you've also been offered the chance to try something new. A new opportunity job is one that involves something completely new—a new area of work related to your field, a new location, or a completely new job.

Michele retired early from her job as a vice president of a credit union. She was 62. She liked the job, but was ready to do something else: namely, travel the world with her husband, who had retired two years prior. She soon learned that her husband was a contented homebody and her travel plans would be forever delayed. When her former job called her back for a short-term project, she was happy to do the work. Months later, she was asked back again to work on something she'd started before retirement that no one had time to finish. After that, she filled in for a departed senior vice president. Then she oversaw the management at new branches. She became the fill-in for jobs needed throughout the company, learned more than she had during her career, and never works more than three days a week. She is expecting to re-retire soon, but she wouldn't be surprised if another project came up before then.

A new opportunity job can be a great way to shift into retirement—it gives you the chance to grow and learn, and there is little to lose. And if you are feeling bored or restless in your current career, a new opportunity job can offer a second chance to do something you truly enjoy.

## The Part-Time Fun Job

This is the earn-enough job I talked about in the introduction to part 2, the avocation or activity you'd almost do for free, if you didn't actually need the cash. Things like working in a tasting room, a bookstore, a ballpark, a theater, an aquarium, or a zoo. We all have at least one fun job we'd probably like to do.

If you need cash, and are reliable and smart, you may be just the type of worker that fun service and entertainment businesses are looking to hire.

Donna worked in retail as a manager for about 30 years and a regional manager for another 13. She was traveling constantly and working at home or in hotels more than 70 hours per week. She decided to get a road hobby, and started writing freelance Web articles for steady money. When the company she was working for closed down, she suddenly found herself looking for something new.

Then she saw a job opening for a position as store manager at a retailer she liked and respected. And it was right near her house. "I decided to interview for the position. I knew the biggest challenge would be stepping so far back, both financially and professionally, but the idea of going to the same place each day and doing something that I knew how to do was extremely appealing. With a job with fewer demands, it would be like being semi-retired. I could actually leave work at work, most of the time," Donna says. The pay was good, she was proud of the product, and she never had to travel or commute. "I loved the job," she says. "I also liked the idea that I could continue to invest for another eight years, until I reached my full retirement age."

Arnold worked long past traditional retirement age, then sold his drapery business after age 70. He still felt agile and capable and wanted something to keep him busy, but despite trying several gigs, nothing lasted long. Then he was offered a job driving new cars to different dealerships throughout Southern California. He had always loved cars and keeping up with the features of the latest makes and models. He enjoyed the long drives in the nice, new cars. Even traffic didn't upset him, because he was getting paid to endure it. The job required keen driving skills, but he could deliver. He could also use the fancy navigation in the new cars to make phone calls, or listen to podcasts and audiobooks. The best part? A few drives per week meant hundreds of extra dollars in his monthly budget.

There's also the part-time job with benefits, which may not be overtly fun, but is a fine choice if you need health insurance. Companies such as Starbucks, Lowe's, Staples, and Whole Foods offer competitive salaries and nice benefits to part-time workers. They may also qualify as fun jobs, depending on who you talk to.

## The Flexible Freelance Job

If you have a skill and very low overhead, you can do freelance work for one or more companies. If you are an editor, designer, teacher, project manager, administrator, data entry expert, or have any number of marketable skills that companies need to farm out, you can make a good living on an hourly or project basis. Sites such as Elance, Upwork, and Freelancer can help you find jobs to launch your freelance career.

Freelance work is similar to consulting work, and it can be done remotely or in-house. How and when you work is typically up to you, as long as you meet the company's deadlines. In some cases, you might be asked to call in to staff meetings.

After a variety of jobs, ranging from university teaching to estate sale prep, Kim entered training to help persons with dyslexia learn to read and study. For over a dozen years she worked for a tutorial agency, and during her last few years with the agency, she was called upon to help students struggling in Latin courses. In retirement, she now works as a freelance tutor in classics (she also volunteers part of the time to help tutor students in need).

Ben was in the US Air Force for 17 years, then worked at a university for 30 years before he retired and began to look for other academic-related activities. He has been "retired" for 19 years, but continues to bring in income from a series of jobs, including online teaching, textbook editing, and lecturing and touring internationally. For him, the travel to more than 30 different countries has been the most exciting thing about his new life as a freelancer.

Bill, a secondary English teacher in the Pittsburgh public schools, retired at 55, the minimum age one could retire and still keep medical benefits. He continues to consult in the field of education, specializing in professional development in literacy. But he also makes money as a digital photographer. He promotes his business online, shows in galleries, and has had great success photographing country music bands for album covers, calendars, and promotional materials.

Freelance offers flexibility that allows you to work when you want and do a variety of things at once. For example, you may spend a few weeks working hourly as a temp or on a long-term consulting project, or you may complete one-off assignments at project rates.

## The Sharing Economy Job

The sharing economy represents the rise of more efficient and individualized service marketing. On the Internet, you can now have practically anything you want, as long as you are willing to pay for it. And if you're one of the people selling your skills, you can find a market for whatever it is you do well. If you enjoy driving or keeping house, you can market and be paid for those tasks. The ability to pet sit or housesit? There's a market for that. If you are looking for short-term jobs or "gigs," the sharing economy helps connect you to people who need your services. And if you sew, make jewelry, or have perfected a recipe for handmade soap, you can easily find a way to sell your goods through Etsy, eBay, or Craigslist.

Judy retired early from a great career in international banking. Over a period of 20 years, she had moved to Arizona with the bank when it was acquired, merged, then acquired again. After the fourth merger, she opted out of a position for which she had been slated. At the age of 44, she received what she calls a "copper parachute"—not exactly golden, but the Arizona version of a nice severance package.

While surfing the Web one day in the 1990s, she found a site called The Mining Company that covered cultural events near Phoenix, where she lived. She didn't like the site and actually wrote to the editors to say she'd be willing to write if they ever needed help. She received a polite, "Thanks, but no thanks." Six months later, she looked at the site again and saw they were hiring for a Phoenix-area writer. She had to compete with other applicants, but she got the job, and has since established one of the largest local tourism sites on the Web.

# The Service-Based Small Business

If you have spent your career dreaming of opening up your own shop, a service business may be the right move for you. It's easier than ever these days to start a small business, and if you have skills that are in demand, you will do well regardless of age or flashy style. Service businesses are relatively simple to set up, with little or no overhead, and they offer flexibility to work at your own pace and during preferred hours.

There is a potential business opportunity in every service under the sun. Common types of service businesses include personal services such as shopping, tutoring, cooking, or cleaning. Pet care services are increasingly popular these days. Business support in the form of editing, translating, bookkeeping, or website management is in demand from companies of all sizes.

Jillian was always known for her organizing abilities, so after a long career in law, she decided to stop working full-time and focus on starting her own personal organizing business. Because she was good at her job, business grew easily through referrals. As she grew, she was able to scale the business and bring on another organizer, allowing the two of them to grow their client base exponentially.

The sharing economy is the latest name for the way people do business on the Internet—using what they have to make other people's lives easier. And earn a nice chunk of cash. Peer-to-peer or interpersonal connections are made securely and easily online; it's a fast and efficient way to find a market for your skills, your house, your car, and even your money. Here are some of the sharing economy opportunities for retirees.

### → ONLINE SERVICE JOB CONNECTIONS

As more sites pop up matching gigs to the workers who need them, it's easier than ever to find small job opportunities online. Services such as TaskRabbit, Fiverr, and Zaarly provide virtual or in-person services to their clients. TaskRabbit mainly looks for people who can do chores, Fiverr focuses on creative services, and Zaarly (which does not operate in every state) offers house maintenance and cleaning. Do you like pet sitting or housesitting? There are sites for that (DogVacay and TrustedHousesitters). If you can write, sites such as About looks for experts in different fields to write Web content on a given topic. Depending on your field, small businesses may also be looking for short-term employees. I don't know of a matchmaking service for that (there's a business idea!) but there will certainly be plenty of job matchmaking services to come as the sharing economy continues to grow.

### → PEER-TO-PEER PROPERTY RENTALS

If you have a home, second home, or vacation home in a desirable area, sites like Airbnb and Homeaway let you market your property for short-term rental.

## → PEER-TO-PEER FINANCING

This includes crowdfunding sites like Kickstarter, AngelList, and GoFundMe, where you can ask others for help in financing a company, charity, invention—you name it.

## → RIDESHARING/ CAR SHARING

If you've ever used Uber, you know the ridesharing service is changing the way we get around, and it's happening around the globe. The company has a special connection to seniors, who are among the business's best clients and most reliable drivers. Half of Uber's drivers are older than 40.[49] Your car must meet their standards and you pass a basic test to get onto their service, but once that's accomplished, you can choose, depending on your schedule, when you are and are not available for riders. Another rideshare company, Lyft, initially tried to be the Uber of carpools, and now it's gaining ground as a competitor, which opens up another line of work. There's also RelayRides if you want to rent out a second car to people looking for a discount rental. Or try Splinster, where you can rent sporting equipment like snowboards, bikes, kayaks, and skis.

All of these sites represent some element of risk. While the organizations that match services and needs try to do what they can to reduce the risk of fraud or crime, they cannot anticipate everything. Nor can they guarantee you will always be hired when you make yourself available. If you are looking for your own jobs on sites like Craigslist, try to protect yourself by getting everything in writing and signed by both parties. As always, remember to be cynical about every promise and resistant to anything that sounds too good to be true.

# The Mission-Driven Nonprofit

There seems to be a point around middle age when we start to seek meaning in our lives and careers. That's the driver of the Encore career movement, where people over 50 are starting careers based on a greater mission or purpose.

Ronald is one such Encore entrepreneur. At 62 years old, Ronald's business was failing. He decided to make a move to another state and was able to find work consulting in his field, which was action sports. While learning more about fundraising for the project, he was introduced to the concept of crowdfunding—that is, using the Internet to raise small amounts of money from large groups of people. He saw an opportunity to use crowdfunding to help support causes, such as local scholarships and loans tied to the community. This led him to found FundOurCommunity, an online platform that matches local nonprofit campaigns with community-oriented support (kind of a small-scale, charitable Kickstarter).[50] The company has made more than $30,000 in community loans, and he hopes to inspire young entrepreneurs with the possibilities that crowdfunding can offer.

There are hundreds of stories like Ronald's on the site Encore.org of people driven to start a nonprofit venture where they see an obvious need. The years before retirement often can be the best time to tackle such a project, when you have the network and resources to make your vision happen.

If you have never worked in a nonprofit environment, it may help to volunteer or intern somewhere to gain experience in the grant process, operations, and other essential areas.

# The Unpaid Volunteer Job

If you don't need the income, unpaid dream jobs may be even easier to come by. Many organizations, including theaters, museums, and other attractions, rely on volunteers to fill holes in their staffing. Volunteering can come with some benefits—free seats to plays, concerts, events, access to exhibits, and backstage schmoozing with celebrities.

Irene spent years as a real estate agent and decorator before retiring with her husband to a small apartment in Manhattan. She spends her time volunteering as a docent at museums throughout the city, including the Museum of Modern Art. Leading tours through the museum involves thorough training, and she must stay sharp and knowledgeable about the art on exhibit. And while hundreds of people compete for docent jobs, it is unpaid. Irene enjoys free admission to the exhibits for friends and family, and a discount at the gift shop, and she values having a personal relationship to the art.

Mary spent her years before retirement working as a school psychologist. After retiring, she went into private practice, taking on a range of clients, some who paid on a sliding-scale according to their means. She also volunteered for CASA (Court-Appointed Special Advocates) on behalf of neglected and abused children. She serves on several committees and is a member of a writing club, senior chorus, book discussion group, and play reading group. Mary still feels as if she has a lot of time on her hands because she sleeps less in her older years.

If you are interested in something really new, there are opportunities to volunteer in other countries. You will be especially valued if you have skills that are in demand in a developing region. Teachers, for example, are needed almost everywhere. There are also a lot of volunteer opportunities helping conserve wildlife in different regions. If you travel with a legitimate nonprofit group, you may be able to deduct a portion of the time spent volunteering from your tax returns. (And you typically don't pay for food or lodging on your trip.)

# The Capital Investing Job

For a select group of people who know what they are doing, investing can be a way to generate income in retirement. This is investing outside of your retirement portfolio, which as a rule shouldn't be used unless you have sufficiently established yourself in an investment and fully understand the risks.

The options for generating income are so vast that it's easy to over-commit in the quest for additional revenue. When you manage your own time, it's important to know the difference between enough and too much.

It is certainly possible to have multiple streams of income from different sources. In fact, it's ideal in terms of diversifying your income. But if it involves work at more jobs than you can handle, you could burn out quickly and hurt your long-term retirement prospects. Allow yourself to grow slowly and steadily, and learn how to identify the best jobs, and how to say "No," to everything else.

Remember the story of my business plan that lacked any real planning? I didn't consider whether I could manage the workload. I just said "Yes" to everything and figured it out later. Often, this was at the expense of my own well-being and/or time with my family. It wasn't good for me and it ultimately wasn't the best experience for my clients. I've since gained a more realistic view of my productivity—I know my limits. It has actually helped my business and my experience working for myself.

The optimal number of new revenue streams after retirement is probably around two for most people. If you plan for two initially, you can get a sense of your own productivity and abilities before you take on too much responsibility. This is a low-stress way to start out on your own.

Investing for retirement income can be done in any number of ways, with varying levels of risk. You could invest in a property that pays steady dividends, such as real estate. You could make small investments in start-up companies, as an angel investor or a friends-and-family investor. You could even day-trade stocks, but only if you are good at it.

The goal is getting to the crossover point—or the point at which your investments start earning more than your expenses. This may also involve reducing expenses to have more capital to save and invest.

Mark made capital investments in several apartment buildings before retirement. Over time, the properties increased in value, and the rent payments have kept up with inflation. After paying mortgages, taxes, insurance, and maintenance on his properties, he is able to live off the income his rentals bring in.

Mark's strategy is known as interest-only. The money he earns in interest is what he spends. This can be done with a more traditional investment portfolio as well, if you can find income investments that pay enough to cover your investments without touching the principal. Individual bonds, dividend-paying stocks, or a fixed deferred annuity are investments that may help you achieve a consistent level of income without touching the principal.

Another investing strategy that has become more popular with the rise of social networking is small-scale angel investing. Angel investing is providing early-stage capital for small business ventures. As banks and traditional lending institutions became stingier after the 2008 credit crisis, angel investors stepped up to fund $22 billion for 65,000 companies in 2011 alone.[51] The site AngelList (angel.co) helps connect investors with start-ups (it even posts start-up jobs if you are looking to become an insider). It can be risky, but if you do the due diligence and find great investments, the rewards can be significant.

You may find the opportunity to invest in a venture for a family member or friend. Friends and family rounds of funding usually offer investors the greatest return on investment. The risk here is allowing emotions or love for your family member cloud your view of the business.

Not everyone can manage investments with confidence. Before making any big investment decisions, seek advice from a professional.

Now that you have a sense of the types of jobs that are out there, are you starting to hone in on your own income opportunities? In the next chapter we'll get more specific about how to start up your new career.

## GET IT DONE

### HAVE YOU . . .

☐ Considered which type of business venture might be the best match for your skills and abilities?

☐ Investigated any phased retirement plans in your company?

☐ Talked to job recruiters about new opportunity jobs or fun jobs that might be available if you made the transition?

☐ Learned more about specific opportunities in your field and the online resources that can help you connect to them?

☐ Reached out to your networks and social networks through sites like LinkedIn to let everyone know your next move?

### RESOURCES

*Repurpose Your Career: A Practical Guide for Baby Boomers* by Mark Miller with Susan Lahey. This book can help you determine a career-changing strategy that works.

*The Encore Career Handbook: How to Make a Living and a Difference in the Second Half of Life* by Marci Alboher. I think Encore careers is a great movement and the organization behind it, Encore.org, is there to support those who want to fulfill their passions in later life. This book can help get you started on your Encore journey.

CollaborativeConsumption.com. This website can help you understand the different categories within the sharing economy—and how to make the most of them.

VolunteerMatch.org. This website can help you find a volunteer opportunity in your area. Or try VolunteerVacations.com or JustGive.org to find information on volunteering abroad.

# CHAPTER SEVEN

# Set Up Shop

Now that you've seen the different types of work available, what seems ideal? You've come a long way since the beginning, and if you've read the chapters and completed the exercises so far, you should be in a good position to start creating revenue streams that you can feel happy about.

As you approach retirement, remember, any work option has to be both engaging and satisfying—and ensure that you'll have sufficient funds and will be able to do the job for many years. In this chapter, we'll talk about the nuts and bolts of getting started on your post- or pseudo-retirement job. If it's been a while since you started a new job, or if your retirement gig will be wildly different from your career, the exercises in this chapter can help you understand what your work might be worth on the open market and calculate how many hours per week you plan to work.

$ _____ × $ _____ = $ _____

    Hourly rate           hours per week         per week

$ _____ × 52 weeks = $ _____

    Hourly rate                               annual rate

# How Much to Charge for Your Work?

Even seasoned professionals have a difficult time determining what to charge for their work. If you are just starting out as a freelancer or consultant, it's a good idea to do some light research to find the going rate for the kind of work you have in mind. If it's a new line of work, you will probably want to begin by charging at the low end of the range that people usually charge, and then, as you gain experience and confidence, you can raise your fee. If you are already very experienced in the type of work you are offering, well, then, you'll want to make sure that your excellent track record is recognized. Eventually, you will need to create your own rules for how you'll price your work. Here are a few questions to ask yourself to get a sense of what you're worth.

- **How much would you make if you did this job full time?**
  If you are familiar with the salary range for someone in your line of work, come up with a comparable hourly rate as a basis for your project. You can also research online salary listings from sites like Salary, Payscale, and Glassdoor. Because you are responsible for your own overhead, you may eventually charge a higher rate than a salaried employer.

> I retired under duress from a company that no longer appreciated experience. They pushed youth ahead of age. They had massive celebrations and parties for people with five and ten years of experience and completely ignored my 30th anniversary. The good news is that after I retired, they had to hire me back. I have made more money more easily and stress-free from consulting in the decade since I retired than I made in the 36 years that I worked at the same company.

LOU, RETIRED IN MARTINS FERRY, OHIO

- **What do you expect to make on the whole project?** You may think of your project in terms of hourly rates to prioritize your time, but present it to a potential client as a flat fee. Some clients may limit the total amount of hours required on a project, but will approve a flat fee that makes sense to them. On the other hand, some clients will insist on an hourly rate. Especially if you are earning an hourly rate, track your time carefully and document your hours in a spreadsheet or calendar. You can also use a time-tracking app like Harvest.

- **What are your expenses?** Don't forget to include costs, such as transportation, research materials, even time spent in meetings, when you determine what to charge for a given project.

- **What's your minimum?** When you price any project, give yourself some wiggle room between your preferred rate and your bottom line. That way, there's room to negotiate and the project is still worthwhile. Once your business is established, set a minimum rate that you will not dip below, regardless of the work.

**S**tarting your own business will likely come with new costs. For example, you may need a faster Internet connection to work on the Web, special software or equipment, tax and incorporation advice, a desk, chair, and filing fees. You will most likely also need the income in the meantime. That's where a bridge job comes in.

A bridge job is something you do until you are ready to start the new venture. It need not be anything fancy, just work that gets you to a place where you can start, without jeopardizing your existing or future savings.

Your current job may be the only bridge you need, if you have the time and energy to start your business in your off hours. If you are already out of work or in retirement and looking for a job or starting a business without an existing income, a bridge job—even one as a barista at Starbucks or a retail sales associate at Staples—can provide a financial cushion while you save your brain for your own business. (The upside is if you're starting a service business, you can learn from companies that know customer service.)

If a client does not want to pay your typical rate, it may be possible instead to pare down the project to do less work for a smaller fee. Either way, do not be afraid to stand firm on your worth. And put the agreed-upon rate in writing, plus a cancellation fee if the work is cancelled on behalf of the client. (One-quarter to one-third of the agreed-upon rate is a good rule of thumb.)

Once you have your hourly rate, you can calculate how many hours per week you need to meet your income needs. If it takes more hours than you anticipated, that should be reflected in your rate in the future. The idea is to work fewer hours, so make sure that your rate compensates for a shorter workweek.

# How Much Income Can You Expect?

Let's take another look at the common paths for work in retirement to get a sense of whether it might be right for you. For each path, we'll look at what to expect, its earning potential, the kind of work-life balance it offers, where to look, and what could go wrong.

# Scaled-Down Day Job

**What to expect?** Your expectations should be based on your needs, unless there are formal or informal programs at your company that allow you to try a flexible schedule, working fewer hours or fewer days in the office. Your company may allow you to shift into part-time or consulting work. Or you may be offered a phased retirement, providing a gradual step-down of hours and responsibilities throughout a period of three to five years.

**Earning potential.** A phased retirement may be reduced work hours at a reduced salary comparable to the one you were making. Expect to make somewhere between half to two-thirds of your current salary, plus benefits.

**Work-life balance factor.** Very balanced. By working 20 to 30 hours per week at your current job, you get a chance to practice retirement part-time and spend more time doing what you love.

**Where to look?** Start with your human resources department to enquire about flexible work arrangements, or ask your manager if it's possible to accommodate a reduced schedule.

**What could go wrong?** If you pursue a phased retirement arrangement at work, discuss the implications for your near- and long-term benefits with your human resources department. The IRS is considering proposed regulations to establish phased retirement guidelines, and the government recently began offering it to employees. At most other employers, these are largely informal, according to the AARP.[52]

# New Opportunity Job

**What to expect?** New opportunity jobs occupy a special category for workers who have a lot of experience, and may be primed to mentor, consult on, or oversee an interesting project. This was a common theme among many of the retirement stories I heard, people being offered interesting opportunities within five to ten years of traditional retirement age. Sometimes the opportunity came randomly; other times it was prompted by an interest or an event, a person taking a class or researching something new, a layoff or early retirement gambit. It's a great option for pre-retirees who want something new but aren't ready to give up the paycheck.

**Earning potential.** Because this job could be anything that's different from what you are doing now, there is no way to get a sense of the rate. The right opportunity might come with a higher salary or a different type of benefit, such as reduced work hours.

**Work-life balance factor.** Depends on the job and what you're looking for. If it's a job that involves working fewer hours, then work-life balance is great. If you get a job requiring more travel, that may be a good or bad thing for balance, depending on your home life and your interest in travel.

**Where to look?** Get a little creative with this one. A new opportunity might come to you if you put some feelers among friends and colleagues in your network. You can also check the job boards at your current employer to explore any new opportunities that can be pursued before retirement. These may include a promotion on a short-term project or new venture, with the option to reevaluate in a year or two. If none are available, reach out to recruiters and other contacts on LinkedIn, and say you are interested in something new. You'd be surprised how much interest a simple message can generate.

If you are still looking for leads, check out large national job websites, such as CareerBuilder, Monster, and SimplyHired, where you can get access to a large volume of general listings. Niche sites like Retirementjobs and Flexprofessionals also have some interesting listings tailored to new opportunity job seekers.

**What could go wrong?** A new opportunity is not always a better opportunity, and you may find this job to be as much as a drudge as the one you started with. The retirees I talked to who have the most success in new opportunity jobs were those who were incredibly interested in the new line of work or new project.

# Part-Time Fun Job

**What to expect?** A lot of job options fall under this umbrella, from working a few hours a week up to 35 hours a week, in an office, retail store, attraction, or entertainment venue. As Rod Sterling used to say, "your only limit is your imagination." It's called a fun job for a reason!

**Earning potential.** Part-time salaries are typically based on full-time salaries divided by the number of hours worked. Some companies pay part-time employees a discounted rate; that is, less than the equivalent full-time salary. On the other hand, because benefits are typically lower for part-time employees, you may get a little extra salary to make up for any benefits you don't get.

If you want a job at a big company, Glassdoor lists hourly rates for part-time workers at some of the biggest and most well-known corporations. Your own salary may vary based on experience, but for budgeting purposes you can stick to national averages, just to be safe.

**Work-life balance factor.** Really good, if you find a job you enjoy and have more free time to do the things you love.

**Where to look?** Visit websites, email, and call companies directly where you want to work. LinkedIn is also a good resource if you know exactly what you are looking for.

Most large job boards have search filters that let you find part-time work in your area of interest and location. Monster, CareerBuilder, and Indeed all list part-time work, and all are good resources if you are looking to work at a large company. Other sites to look at include Flexjobs, where you will find a surprising amount of professional part-time, flexible full-time, or telecommuting jobs. The site verifies the legitimacy of the jobs it posts, so you are less likely to get scammed. You'll have to pay a monthly fee of around $15 to access the listings, which could be a good investment if it leads to steady work.

Backdoorjobs specializes in "short-term adventures," and you'll find a lot of summer camp jobs listed there. Look beyond that for opportunities to work and teach abroad. The website CoolJobs lists a lot of fun seasonal work. Despite the teenage summer camp pictures, there really are great jobs listed there for you. Or try SnagaJob, which lists only hourly work. If there are specialized sites in your area of interest, investigate those for part-time opportunities. And Craigslist is a must for finding interesting gigs.

Keep in mind, when interviewing, it's important to go in with a sense of the general schedule you'd like to keep or amount of hours you are looking for, and stick to it. You can be flexible, if you think you can handle it, but you should also set limits on your time. Remember, you are making these changes for a reason.

**What could go wrong?** Part-time jobs don't typically offer benefits, so you're better off with COBRA, Medicare, or private insurance. On the upside, you may qualify for unemployment benefits if you get laid off or let go.

## Flexible Freelance Job

**What to expect?** Freelancing and consulting are common ways to work these days. Just more than a third of the US workforce is freelancing, either as a primary source of income or a side job.[53] If you haven't tried it yet, it's pretty easy to hang a proverbial shingle and start getting work. You may even be able to transition out of your current job with regular freelance assignments or projects. If it's flexibility and freedom you want, a freelance job can be whatever you make it.

I use the terms *freelancer* and *consultant* interchangeably, but there are some distinctions between the two. Consultants usually spend a lot of time on site when working on a job. Freelancers tend to work independently. Consultants are usually providing a high level of expertise, knowledge, or skill to an organization, whereas freelancers are project workers. Call yourself whatever you want, it's not likely to come up with your clients.

**Earning potential.** A massive global survey of more than 23,000 freelancers across the world found that the average freelancer works 36 hours a week and earns about $21 per hour.[54] But those are global averages, and your rate will depend on the job, your skill level, and average rates in your field. If you're handy on social networks, brand yourself as an expert in a field to gain credibility and clients.

**Work-life balance factor.** Could lean a little too far toward work, if you don't manage your time and workload.

**Where to look?** Current freelancer favorites include LocalSolo, Freelancer, Upwork, Elance, and Traction. Sites cater to different markets, so explore more than one to get noticed by the widest possible audience. Whatever kind of work you do, try to create some sort of online portfolio or presence using a site like Tumblr or a visual site like Dunked.

If you fancy yourself more of the consultant type, there are sites designed just for you. Guru lets you market your guru skills in areas like accounting, legal, IT, and engineering. The site acts as a third-party administrator between you and the client (many staffing firms work this way, as well). Skillbridge.co (notice it's ".co" and not ".com") is a site for "business freelancers" who have advanced degrees and have worked at elite firms. Creative types can use sites like Behance, for graphic and visual designers, artists, and illustrators.

**What could go wrong?** You may have lots of work sometimes and not much work at other times, so budget a little extra for savings when times are good. It's also easy to overextend yourself and wind up working harder than ever.

# Sharing Economy Job

**What to expect?** What'dya got? Want to sell it? Or at least rent it? That's the premise of the sharing economy. People everywhere are selling or renting things they already possess as a means of bringing in income. That sounds a lot less creepy than it might have 10 or 20 years ago. In fact, the sharing economy can be a boon for seniors.

# THE BUSINESS OF BABYSITTING

**D**o you want a job working with gorgeous, fabulous people you happen to be obsessed with? If you can handle the spills, smells, eardrum-piercing screams, and eye rolls, then professional babysitting may be right for you. If you have grandchildren, you may be able to score steady work providing child care, tutoring, after-school transportation, and other services so in demand by today's busy parents.

Babysitting is a common pastime for retired grandparents. An estimated 30 percent of preschool-age kids with working mothers receive child care from a grandparent, according to the US Census Bureau. It's a good bet not all of those doting grandparents get paid, but you should.

## → TAKE YOURSELF SERIOUSLY

You love your children and want to help, but if you need to earn money at this job, that should be part of the deal. Negotiate an hourly, weekly, or monthly rate that works for you and the parents, and try to hold them to it.

## → TAKE THE JOB SERIOUSLY

If you're going to be a professional, you should act like one. Pay attention to the parents' rules and try not to let your grandparent instincts get the best of you.

## → TACKLE PROBLEMS BEFORE THEY FESTER

Communication can be strange among family members, which gets in the way of professional relationships. There is no way around this except to deal with issues as they arise and try not to get too emotional about the little things.

**Earning potential.** Depending on what you have to offer and how much you put into participating, you can make real money. A recent article in *TheStreet* covered people earning six-figure incomes from the sharing economy.[55]

**Work-life balance factor.** Good. You turn more aspects of your life into work, but the time commitment will likely be much more flexible. And if you really become a sharing economy pro, you could find ways to farm out your work to others at a lower price.

**Where to look?** On Yerdle you can sell anything, although the site works by "swapping" your items for Yerdle dollars, which you then use to buy other's people's stuff on the site. On TaskRabbit you can sell your time, patience, and skills; for example, picking up and delivering dry cleaning or installing shelves. Fiverr lets you hawk your creative skills, from composing a song to making videos using puppets. RelayRides lets you rent out your car. Or you can join Uber or Lyft, and after a minimal training period, rent out your driving skills. You can rent your home, vacation home, or a room in your home on HomeAway or Airbnb. I think of Etsy and Ebay and Craigslist as sharing economy sites, as well, where you can literally sell anything. By the time you read this book, there are probably 20 new sites that let you buy, sell, or rent more of the same. I distinguish the sharing economy jobs from freelance jobs, but you could have more than one of each at the same time.

**What could go wrong?** A lot of sharing can get tiresome, especially if strangers are constantly in your space.

# Service-Based Small Business

**What to expect?** More than 5 million people age 55 or older own small businesses, according to the Small Business Administration. One research firm found that about one-third of all small-business owners in the United States are age 65 or older.[56] I think that means you are part of a hot market segment.

The ease in which you start up and become successful will depend on many things, including the type of service you want to provide compared to demand in the marketplace. Once you have an idea, it's important to evaluate where you stand against the competition. Typically, you'll want to analyze the strengths and weaknesses of your potential business, as well as what opportunities exist that might support your business and threats that might make it harder for your business to catch on. (Business schools call this a SWOT analysis, which is an acronym for Strengths, Weaknesses, Opportunities, Threats.) You may also want to write a business plan, which is a great first step and can help you define your vision, and is a necessity if you want to get funding and launch nationally. You can start by selling your services part-time, to get a sense of what the work will be like. The Small Business Administration (SBA.gov) is a great resource if you want to know more about becoming an entrepreneur.

**Earning potential.** It can take a business a few months to get off the ground, and success and profitability will depend on a number of factors. But if it's a service business with low overhead, you can start taking profits right away.

**Work-life balance factor.** Terrible. Entrepreneurs are known to work too much and love it.

**Where to look?** You should decide on a business structure and open a business bank account as soon as you book your first gigs. This will make tax time much easier. There may be legal requirements for you to start your business. Any permits, licenses, or certificates necessary in your industry should be included in your upfront costs.

Marketing your services may at first feel a lot like looking for a job. You have to have a resume or strong brand message, and be able to sell what sets you apart from the competition. Networking and referrals is a good place to start. Get the message out to everyone you know (and everyone they know) that you are doing this work and looking for customers. Marketing and advertising to a larger client base may also make sense, but if you are going to spend money on it, do a little research on what is most effective for your type of business. Sometimes you can even find related business owners who are interested in partnerships and deals to share mutual clients and referrals.

## 6 QUESTIONS TO ASK YOURSELF BEFORE STARTING YOUR OWN BUSINESS

1. Do you have the resources to start the business (or a bridge job to support you until the business turns a profit)?

2. What is the potential income that can be generated by this business?

3. Do you have the experience or special skills that stand out in this business? What is the value you add to the work?

4. Can you physically handle the strains of the business?

5. How much do you need to earn? How long will it take to become profitable?

6. Will you enjoy the work?

Marketing and promotion will depend on the business you are in, but it's easy to promote locally for free on sites like Yelp, Google Reviews, Facebook, Instagram, and Twitter. Depending on the area, local promotion boards and spaces may be a good idea, Craigslist has an impact in most areas, or you could go the old-fashioned route and put an ad in the local paper.

**What could go wrong?** You may function as your own accounts receivables department, which means you have to make sure you get paid. This can be the hardest part about running your own business.

## HOW MUCH MONEY DO YOU NEED TO START A SMALL BUSINESS?

I've read articles about how you can start a business for an average $30,000, $3,000, or $30. All answers are true, it just depends on your business and the overhead involved.

Some of your start-up costs—including rent, advertising, staffing, and training—may be tax deductible, up to around $5,000 in your first year, according to the SBA.[57]

If your business requires a lot of upfront expense, you can look into a small business loan. But be careful not to risk your retirement assets as collateral.

# Mission-Driven Nonprofit

**What to expect?** Nonprofits, also called charitable organizations or educational companies, typically require people with the same types of skills needed at other companies, but you can feel the work you do is for a greater good. Nonprofit jobs can be just as competitive as any other job, and they hire in the same way that typical companies do.

If you are starting a nonprofit from scratch, you need to treat it as seriously as a business. That means having a business plan and a plan for profitability. You'll also need to file for tax-exempt status and create bylaws for how you will incorporate.

**Earning potential.** How much income you will earn from a nonprofit may be trickier to determine. Salaries are generally comparable to private-company pay rates. If you run your own nonprofit, your salary should fall under the category of administrative costs and should generally not exceed 10 percent of total donor dollars. It probably goes without saying that, if you're in it for the money, a nonprofit may not be the way to go.

However, while nonprofit employees do get paid, volunteers do not. But I'm including volunteers in this category because the jobs (and the motivations) are often found in the same places.

**Work-life balance factor.** Heavy on the work. There's a level of commitment that leads people to work for a nonprofit. People in nonprofit careers are typically driven by a mission and put everything they can into the work.

**Where to look?** Nonprofits advertise jobs on the same broad job boards used by private and public companies. So use job sites such as Indeed, CareerBuilder, or LinkedIn, or use your personal network to try and find general opportunities. Then you can dig into sites that serve the nonprofit space, including Philanthropy, Idealist.org, and Encode. OpportunityKnocks.org caters to people "who want to change the world." The Council of Nonprofits lists jobs with charitable organizations by state, and you can find New York City jobs on NYNP.biz.

**What could go wrong?** "Nonprofit burnout" is an industry buzzword. These jobs can be just as demanding as any for-profit job, but with the added burden of saving the world.

# Unpaid Volunteer Job

**What to expect?** Volunteering is a way to connect and give to your community. You can also use volunteer work strategically, as a way to learn new skills or make connections in an area or industry. Even if you're just in it for the social life opportunities, you're making a difference while you're making friends.

**Earning potential.** Did I mention this was unpaid work? There is the possibility to try and deduct a portion of your car and travel expenses, and out-of-pocket expenses from your taxes. There may also be fringe benefits, like memberships or invites to fundraising parties. Volunteering can give you experience and contacts in a new career, which may lead to paid work.

**Work-life balance factor.** Excellent. You determine the hours, and it doesn't impact your income. This should be work that makes you feel happy and fulfilled, or else you probably won't continue to do it. Speaking of happiness, studies have found that helping others kindles happiness. There's even a phrase for the rush you get from doing something good for others: "helper's high."

**Where to look?** VolunteerMatch is one of the largest job sites. Idealist.org also lists volunteer opportunities. The Me To We site is all about volunteer trips (http://www.metowe.com/volunteer-travel/). And sites like CatchaFire.org and the HandsOnNetwork.org are designed to match your skills with organizations in need.

**What could go wrong?** Your first (or second, or third) experience may not be the best volunteering experience. It takes tenacity to stick with it and find a cause and a job that you can enjoy.

## ALIGN YOUR WORK-LIFE CHI

**I**'ve recently become a fan of acupuncture. Those needles hit a few right spots, and I can feel my body find its natural balance. With a few precise moves, you can readjust your work-life balance and make your life easier, regardless of what you do in retirement.

### → PLAN YOUR LIMITS

If you've decided you want to work only 20 hours per week in retirement, treat it as a firm rule. Don't let yourself get overwhelmed with work, or you risk ending up as overworked and miserable as you were in your 9-to-5.

### → STICK TO A SCHEDULE

Set regular work hours for yourself, even if you work at home. By keeping a daily routine, you train yourself to be productive during certain hours, so you can relax the rest of the time.

### → LEARN TO SAY "NO"

When you rely on multiple streams of income for your livelihood, you want to accept every opportunity that comes your way. But you can do only so much; accepting too much work can be bad for you and it's not great for the work you produce.

### → ADJUST AS YOU LEARN

If you do get overwhelmed, adjust your workload so that it doesn't happen again. Learn from your mistakes, so you can form better productivity habits.

### → GIVE YOURSELF PLENTY OF VACATIONS

Not just vacations, but field trips, long lunches, mental health days, and as much free time as you need to keep yourself in balance, always. Be that employee who isn't trying to impress everyone with anything but competence and skill.

# Capital Investing Job

**What to expect?** Unless you have a solid track record day trading stocks, I wouldn't go in that direction. Instead, it makes sense to look for dividend-paying investments, including real estate and rental properties, and dividend-paying exchange-traded funds that throw off monthly income.

**Earning potential.** Historically, the market has returned about 8 percent per year on average. You may make much more in a given year, or much less, but plan for years when the market (whatever market you are investing in) is not your friend. It's great during years when investments perform better than that, but this should be steady, boring income without a lot of risk.

**Work-life balance factor.** Great, unless you have a volatile market without a backup plan. If you have the technology, you can check on your investments from your beachside cabana.

**Where to look?** Take advantage of free resources on brokerage and industry Internet sites, which can teach you a lot about being an investor. Head over to Kahn Academy and you'll feel like an expert in no time. Confidence is key for a professional investor, and that comes with having an understanding of the markets, diversification, low-fee investing, and risk.

**What could go wrong?** A financial meltdown of *epic* proportions, or even a bad year, can turn your stomach.

# Does It Impact Social Security?

If you work while collecting Social Security benefits, your monthly amount may be reduced before full retirement age.

If you are younger than full retirement age and make more than the yearly earnings limit ($15,720 in 2016), Social Security deducts $1 in benefits for every $2 you earn above that amount. If you are within a year of full retirement age, Social Security deducts $1 for every $3 you earn above a higher limit ($41,880 in 2016). But if your benefits are reduced, they'll come back to you in the form of higher future benefits.

If your income increases in the years before taking Social Security, it can impact your benefit. Social Security reviews your records annually and recalculates your benefit amount if it should be higher. The same is not necessarily true if your income decreases in the years before retirement. If you have a strong work record, the years before retirement should not impact your average on the downside, but be on the safe side and verify it using Social Security's retirement estimator calculator (ssa.gov/estimator) before making any extreme career decisions.

## GET IT DONE

### HAVE YOU . . .

☐ Estimated how much income you might expect from different sources?

☐ Determined how you will structure your working life in retirement?

☐ Calculated the impact that working may have on Social Security benefits?

### RESOURCES

*Unretirement: How Baby Boomers Are Changing the Way We Think About Work, Community, and the Good Life* by Chris Farrell. This book, by NPR expert and host of the Unretirement podcast (www.infiniteguest.org/unretirement/), provides an overview of different types of careers in the "unretirement" phase.

Workers 50+ Phased Retirement and Flexible Retirement Arrangements (assets. aarp.org/www.aarp.org_/articles/money/employers/phased_retirement.pdf). This online brochure from the American Association of Retired Persons (AARP) provides strategies for phased retirement.

Getting Benefits While Working (https://www.ssa.gov/planners/retire/whileworking .html). Find out more about what happens to your Social Security benefits when you earn income.

SBA.gov. The SBA is a great resource for small business information, funding through loans and grants, and finding contracting work. And they offer detailed advice for opening specific types of service businesses (gym, child care, nonprofit, etc.).

# CHAPTER EIGHT

# Reality Check

At some point while reading this book, you may have asked yourself, "Really? Is this plan going to work?" It's an excellent question, because to ask it means you are taking this seriously, you want to test the veracity of this plan. How very smart of you.

Here's the thing: I can't answer it. It's a question only you can answer. We can assume I think it's going to work, because I'm the one offering you the blueprint and telling you what's possible. I can also tell you that other retirees have made this blueprint work. But your participation is crucial. The one factor I can't predict is you. Only you can make the plan work.

Still, I'm happy to indulge your inner skeptic by offering a little downside risk management. In this chapter, you will reevaluate your initial plan based on everything you've learned so far. Knowing what you know now, it's time to reexamine the budget, take another look at expected income, and see how the pieces fit together.

This is also the time to face potential pitfalls. What is most likely to throw you off your budget? What are the greatest barriers to your revenue streams? How will you handle problems you encounter?

# The Important Power of Setbacks

No one is saying it will be a cakewalk getting a new job or, for that matter, starting a business or charity after you retire. There may be setbacks if you decide to pursue something new. I sympathize; believe me, I have encountered my fair share.

But I have also seen what is possible for people who have the right plan and who are willing to put in some work. Not all freelance and part-time gigs are great, but if you land the right one, you could bring in a nice, regular paycheck. The sharing economy could be a giant headache and may even cost you until you figure out how to make the most of the online service you use. Plenty of businesses fail in their early years, but a business with little overhead (basically you in a chair with a laptop and a WiFi password) wouldn't need to generate a ton of money for you to call it a success. All you'd need would be one or two steady jobs, and you are off and running.

Setbacks are going to happen, in this process and others: from the tantrum-inducing to life-altering, all setbacks feel like the worst setback ever. Even those we know are ultimately for the best—even those feel crappy; particularly for someone like me, who is far more likely to take negative criticism to heart than positive feedback. The upside is that I pay so much attention to the negative that I've learned more from my setbacks than from my triumphs.

We all learn from setbacks and often end up in a better place because of them. But to increase your odds, this chapter will offer specifics on how to anticipate, reframe, and overcome potential setbacks in retirement.

If your plan is still not quite coming together, adjustments can be made. Remember the different levers that can be pulled to get your adjustment right? It's time to revisit those: spend less, earn more, or save more.

# Spend Less

One of the greatest threats to your retirement success is your own spending. If retirement to you means golf courses, country club lunches, and beach vacations, you will either be disappointed or you will very soon be broke.

Instead, focus on those things that made you so happy in chapter 1: having more free time, seeing family and friends, focusing on what's important to you. The tradeoff is that you might have to live on less than you did before, but you might find that easier to do than you'd think.

### WORKSHEET 8.1 **BUDGET REDO, REDUX**

Remember the budget that you worked and reworked back in Part 1? I want you to revisit it with a more ruthless eye. Can you cut nonessentials and further reduce your monthly expenses?

Look at the current cost and potential ways to reduce each item in your budget. Move items from one column to the other as necessary.

| BUDGET ITEM | COST | WAYS TO REDUCE? | NEW COST |
|---|---|---|---|
| Mortgage/rent | $ | | $ |
| Water/power | $ | | $ |
| Phone/cable/Internet | $ | | $ |
| Home maintenance | $ | | $ |
| Loan/debt servicing | $ | | $ |
| Car payment | $ | | $ |
| Car insurance | $ | | $ |

| BUDGET ITEM | COST | WAYS TO REDUCE? | NEW COST |
| --- | --- | --- | --- |
| Public transportation | $ | | $ |
| Gas | $ | | $ |
| Groceries | $ | | $ |
| Insurance | $ | | $ |
| Prescriptions, medical out of pocket | $ | | $ |
| Misc. | $ | | $ |
| Income tax | $ | | $ |
| Property tax | $ | | $ |
| Savings | $ | | $ |
| Dining out | $ | | $ |
| Clothing | $ | | $ |
| Hobbies | $ | | $ |
| Entertainment | $ | | $ |
| Vacations/travel | $ | | $ |
| Big-ticket purchases | $ | | $ |
| Charitable contributions | $ | | $ |

➤ Expenses total per month $ _____ × 12 months

➤ New annual expenses total $ _____

> We live on a strict and tight budget. Everything is budgeted, including savings each month toward upcoming anticipated costs like medical, car repairs, taxes, heat, electric, concerts, eating out, and miscellaneous.
>
> CAPERTON, RETIRED IN SARANAC LAKE, NEW YORK

# Tips to Live Like a Cheapskate

When it comes to saving money in retirement, the best ideas come from actual retirees. That's why I love to read the comments accompanying any article about saving money in retirement (and there are plenty, as a quick Google search will prove). The trick is to cherry-pick the best ideas and avoid anything too extreme (or dangerous). Here are some of the best ideas I've found for living like a cheapskate in retirement.

- **Spend less time shopping.** This is different than spending less when you shop. By spending less time at the store, you reduce your chances of overspending. Even if you limit your shopping to the grocery store, it makes sense to go less often and maximize the trip.

- **Embrace senior discounts.** Fans of 2000s-era *Saturday Night Live* may recall Molly Shannon's character, Sally O'Malley, whose catchphrase was a loud and proud, "I'm 50!" That's how I imagine you asking for a discount at your favorite stores, restaurants, or attractions: with fearless, self-entitled pride. Don't be afraid to ask for any senior discount you are entitled to—even if you don't see any indication that a discount is offered.

- **Use coupons.** The Internet has made couponing easier than ever for those who have the time and will to keep up with them. If you shop less and plan your shopping trips, it's easier to incorporate coupons and deals in your area. Coupons.com is a great source to start with and even has apps to help you find deals on the go.

- **If you use credit cards, make them rewards cards.** Credit cards can be trouble if you carry a large balance from month to month. But if you regularly pay off your balance, using the right credit card to pay for everyday expenses can really be a boon. Today's rewards cards offer travel perks, cash back on purchases, even signing bonuses. Sites like NerdWallet and CreditKarma can help you compare the latest and greatest offerings.

- **Favor the free.** Free stuff is all around, if you know where to look. You can ditch your telephone and make free long-distance calls via Gmail. Use the library for books, magazine subscriptions, and DVD rentals. Keep up with community websites and newsletters to find free events, entertainment, and exercise classes. Meetup.com is good for finding free classes and groups. If you want to save money on home improvement, check out free workshops at the Home Depot. There are even free generic drugs programs through major retailers including Walmart and Meijer.

## Consider a Home Downsize

If your house seems large for your post-kid lifestyle, downsizing may make sense, depending on the size of your space, your equity, and your needs. If you can find a nice place at a fraction of the cost you pay now, you can cut a big chunk out of your essential monthly expenses. You can also save a ton on heating, cooling, and maintenance costs. Here are four questions to ask yourself about downsizing your space.

1. **Are there less-expensive living options?**

   If you have owned your home for a long time, you may have a good deal of wealth locked up in your home equity, but you also probably have a low monthly house payment. Before making any move, ensure that there are more affordable housing options available to you. Remember also to factor in taxes, maintenance, and home-owner or condo association fees. Your housing costs should be less than 30 percent and ideally closer to 25 percent of your after-tax income.

> Plan to cash in on all the assets that are all around you—all that stuff in the attic, garage, and basement you have been intending to get rid of can be sold on Craigslist and eBay or at a yard sale. Make day one of retirement the beginning of making money. Plus, it gives you something to do during the transition.
>
> JOHN, RETIRED IN THOUSAND OAKS, CALIFORNIA

2. **Is this the right market to sell?**

   Generally, it doesn't make sense to let market conditions dictate your decisions, but in real estate those conditions really count. The bad news is you can't always trust the comparable home price estimates on Internet sites like Zillow and Trulia. But your local real estate professional will gladly give you a free estimate for how much your house is worth on the current market.

3. **Have you budgeted for realtor costs, closing costs, and moving expenses?**

   As a rule of thumb, you should take 10 percent off the top of any profit made from the sale of your property to cover expenses related to the sale and move. Does the prospect of a move still make sense once you factor in these costs?

4. **Can you adapt to your new space?**

   This question is crucial. You want to move to a place that supports your retirement lifestyle and where you can thrive. Is the layout of the home comfortable for daily living? Do you need a room where your children or grandchildren can stay when they visit? Try to find a place where you will still be able to live in 10, 20, or 30 years from now. That means tri-level homes with spiral staircases, for example, are probably out. A bedroom and a bathroom on the first floor can be an excellent investment for the long term.

# Lower Your Taxes

Taxes are expenses that seem hard to control, but there are things to do to lower your tax bill. For example, if you decide to move, you can further lower your expenses by finding a low tax state. But be sure to balance a state's tax rate with the level of service it provides for its residents.

- **Federal income tax.** Federal income tax rates can vary according to how much you bring in each year, anywhere from zero to 39.6 percent of your adjusted gross income. Because retirees live on less income, they typically pay less in income taxes.

- **Capital gains tax.** If you earn income from stocks, bonds, and real estate, you pay capital gains taxes on the income, which are between zero and 20 percent, depending on your income. For most of us, the capital gains rate is 15 percent.

- **Property tax.** Nobody enjoys paying home property taxes each year. In certain swank suburbs, the property levies are astronomical. While it's generally difficult to compare property taxes from one region to another, certain states stand out for their high rates. If you're planning to move to a different state when you retire, you should take that state's property tax into consideration. The top five highest property tax states in 2015 were New Jersey, Illinois, New Hampshire, Connecticut, and Wisconsin. The lowest property tax states were Hawaii, Alabama, Louisiana, Delaware, and D.C.

- **State tax.** Seven states—Alaska, Texas, Washington, Nevada, South Dakota, Florida, and Wyoming—have no state income tax. Tennessee and New Hampshire are states that only tax dividend income. The majority of the other states allow retirees to exclude their pension and Social Security income from taxes.

- **Sales tax.** The taxes you pay on purchases can add up, especially when buying big-ticket items. California has the highest sales tax of 7.5 percent. Alaska, Delaware, New Hampshire, Oregon, and Montana have no state sales tax (although within Alaska and Montana, local regions may be able to impose taxes). Colorado's is the lowest nonzero tax among the states, at 2.9 percent.

**I**f you spend any time on the Internet, you may be familiar with the trend of tiny houses. They are basically portable living spaces that fit everything one needs into an area that's less than 400 square feet, and they're apparently becoming quite popular among millennials and retirees alike (although not so popular that the sales are tracked). The houses are adorable, if a bit extreme. But could you live in such a small space?

Whether you opt for a tiny house or just one that's tinier than the one you had before, making a move to a smaller space can mark the start of a new lifestyle in retirement. Here are some of the benefits of adapting to a smaller space.

### ✦ CHEAPER UTILITIES

With less square footage to heat and cool, your energy bills should go down. Ditto for your property taxes.

### ✦ LESS CLUTTER

Possibly more painful than downsizing your space is the task of downsizing your stuff. But a small space forces you to do it. If you've always wanted a Zen lifestyle, a smaller space is a good first step. Have an epic yard sale and add the money to your savings.

### ✦ EASIER TO CLEAN

There's less surface area to sweep, dust, and scrub in a smaller space. And the constraints will keep you from adding clutter in the future.

### ✦ ENVIRONMENTALLY FRIENDLIER

Easier to heat, cool, and clean means better for the planet, too. Even if it means nothing to you, it's a bonus for Mother Earth.

### ✦ BETTER MANEUVERABILITY

You may be spry and physically capable now, but in the future there may be limitations on your mobility. It may be easier to get around with less space to move through and, ideally, fewer floors.

# Earn More: Increase Your Income

There is still time to adjust earnings expectations from your next job. But in the meantime, let's discuss your savings withdrawal rate. Remember the rate at which you decided to spend down your retirement accounts, earlier on in the book? It's time to stress test that as well, to arrive at a sustainable rate for your portfolio and your budget.

## CAN YOU MAINTAIN YOUR WITHDRAWAL RATE?

Your savings withdrawal rate is the key to retirement success or failure. Draw down your savings too quickly, and you run the risk of running out of money.

If you decide to set the rate at 4 percent, you also need to decide if that amount is fixed or will adjust with inflation. If you have a $200,000 portfolio, your withdrawal in the first year would be $8,000. If you go with an inflation-adjusted rate, the next year you would take the same $8,000 plus inflation, and so on. If you go with a fixed rate, you will take 4 percent of the portfolio, regardless of inflation.

What could go wrong?

- **You need more than 4 percent.** Say you need to generate $16,000 in income from your portfolio each year but you have only $200,000 in savings. You would be drawing down your account at an 8 percent rate, about twice as quickly as financial experts recommend. But if you can find investments that earn money for you, that may help supplement your income without impacting the principal of your portfolio. This is where an investment adviser comes in handy, to help figure out feasible ways to bridge income gaps.

- **Your portfolio falls in value.** During volatile market periods, your savings could lose a significant portion of its value, and in those years you may have to withdraw more than 4 percent. So if your portfolio starts at $200,000 and you take $8,000 in the first year, then the next year your portfolio falls in value to $150,000,

4 percent of which is $6,000. But you need at least $8,000, plus inflation, to live. This is where the risk comes in. On the flip side, in years when your portfolio grows more than expected, you may be able to increase your spending rate.

- **You live too long.** Your time horizon is a big factor in the safety of your withdrawal rate. It's impossible to know exactly how long you will live, but you can check life-expectancy tables or, if you're in your 60s, assume longevity of 20 to 30 years. If you have a longer time horizon, 4 percent or less is a safe bet. But if you are retiring at an older age, you may be able to take a higher rate.

- **You have the wrong asset allocation.** The analysis behind the 4 percent rule assumed a portfolio with equal percentage weighting in stocks and bonds (50/50). You may veer from this slightly, but if you have zero equities, it's not going to be easy to maintain your withdrawal rate, especially in the recent interest-rate environment.

- **You retire in a bad year.** This is different from your portfolio falling in value, although that will happen in this instance. But retiring in a bad year can set off something known as sequence of returns or sequence risk. Say the market knocks your $200,000 portfolio down to $150,000, which gives you $6,000 in the first year, a far cry from the $8,000 you were anticipating. If your withdrawal rate has to compensate for negative performance because you retire during a bear market, the sustainability of your portfolio is at risk. Withdrawing fixed percentage amounts without inflation adjustments can help reduce this risk.

- **Inflation gets ugly.** Inflation is low by historical standards, yet a group called the Senior Citizens League recently found that seniors have lost nearly a third of their buying power since 2000.[58] That means your portfolio has to work harder to keep up with your income needs.

S ome setbacks are more difficult to overcome than others. Here are some difficult situations you may face as a retiree.

### ✈ BECOMING SOCIALLY WITHDRAWN

One big reason to stay in the workforce is to spend time around coworkers, friends, and associates. In retirement, it's much easier to avoid people—which is a bad thing. We need people, even annoying coworker and client types, to keep us mentally nimble and responsive. That's why it's important to keep in touch with friends and family members, stay active on social networks like Facebook and Twitter, join a book or wine club, and generally spend enjoyable time around other people.

### ✈ EXPOSING YOURSELF TO PREDATORS

Those episodes of Dr. Phil? The ones where the stubborn senior defends his or her decision to wire money to an online fling who happens to live on the other side of the planet? Please do not end up one of those people. I hope it sounds obvious that if you meet the love of your life on the Internet and he or she is stuck and unable to access money, you will know what to do: run.

Falling in love with an Internet predator is not the only scam that can separate you from your money. You could have your identity stolen or have someone you trust steal your money.

Keeping yourself from predators may seem difficult, but it really boils down to common sense. For example, the Internal Revenue Service is unlikely to call or email an individual asking for a back payment. As a reporter, I know that it's difficult to get the IRS on the phone, let alone get email attention from the busy agency. If someone is investigating, suing, or even simply questioning you at a government agency or a corporation, they will more than likely notify you in writing. Don't fall for a phone solicitation that promises to make you rich or reward you with a free trip to the Bahamas—provided you hand over your Social Security number. In fact, be wary of giving out your Social Security number to anyone who asks.

The Federal Trade Commission keeps up with the latest scams and shares them on its consumer scam alerts page (www.consumer.ftc.gov /scam-alerts). And pay attention to the concerns of friends and relatives who might suspect something is wrong. If they have to take you on Dr. Phil, you've probably been scammed.

## ➤ IGNORING HEALTH ISSUES

Prevention is said to be the best medicine. It's also the cheapest. Stay on top of potential or existing health problems, and it's likely to cost you less to avoid or manage them. Thanks to the Affordable Care Act, annual checkups and many routine exams are covered by health insurance without additional cost. However, unavoidable health issues increase as we age. Your retirement plan should make allowances should you develop long-term health issues.

## ➤ HIRING THE WRONG ADVISERS

Bad advice can be detrimental to your plan. Don't trust advisers who promise outsize returns (e.g., "I'll double your money.") or talk mostly about themselves and their track record. Instead, look for a professional who is a fee-based, certified financial planner designee, meaning they charge fees for investment advice instead of earning commissions on investments they sell. It's also important to find an adviser who is a fiduciary, meaning they are obligated to put your interests first. It's an important distinction, because nonfiduciaries may seem like they are acting on your behalf, but instead they are profiting from your decisions.

CONTINUED ▸▸

## ✦ PAYING TOO MUCH TO INVEST

Even little fees, the extra 1 percent here and there, can add up. You don't notice them when you are accumulating your savings, but when you need it to generate income, you start to pay attention. So if you're paying an expense ratio of more than 1 to 1.5 percent for a given investment, investigate what that investment adds to your portfolio and whether you can get that exposure for less.

## ✦ IGNORING STOCKS

One thing about getting older is you remember more of the bad markets. Rampant inflation in the 1970s. The savings and loan crisis in the 1980s. The tech stock bubble of the 1990s. The housing and banking collapse of 2008. As bad as those events were, the US stock market has still returned about 10 percent per year since the beginning of the 20th century.[59] Don't let those nasty markets taint your entire investing experience. Your portfolio needs some exposure to equities to achieve growth and beat inflation.

## ✦ LOSING A SPOUSE

There's no way around the emotional loss, but if you depend on the earnings of your spouse, make sure you have a plan for what to do if one of you dies. Life insurance should be in place to cover income gaps, and you should have a sense of which benefits you will continue to receive from your spouse's working record.

Pensions typically offer recipients a choice between a higher, single-life benefit, which ends when you die, and a lower joint or survivor benefit, which continues to pay a portion for the duration of your spouse's life. You may also qualify for Social Security survivor's benefits, so determine how much income that will be, as well.

# Putting Your House in Order

Estate planning is one of those areas of finance that sounds too fancy for most people. When you're struggling to make the monthly rent or mortgage payment, you're probably not thinking the word *estate* applies to you. But estate planning is more about the "estate" of you. And we could all use a set of instructions.

It's important for everyone to have an estate plan, regardless of your age or income level. To be sure, the estate tax impacts only individuals or families with estates valued at more than $5.45 million in 2016. If you have that level of assets, you should probably seek advice from a financial adviser or estate-planning attorney. For the rest of us, estate planning is really about inheritance and instructions for what happens when we can no longer express ourselves due to illness, injury, or death.

## 5 ESTATE PLANNING MOVES TO MAKE NOW

For most of us, estate planning boils down to a few important decisions and documents. While there's no deadline to complete or update these before you retire, pre-retirement is a great time to check these off your list.

1. **Review your beneficiaries.**

   A lot of our assets are held in accounts that have beneficiaries listed on them. These include IRAs, 401(k) plans, Roths, insurance policies, annuities. You name beneficiaries when you open the accounts, and if you haven't checked who is listed on yours in a while, now is a good time. It's easy enough to check in with account managers and update your beneficiaries so that your money will flow where you want after your death.

2. **Draft a will.**

   For assets that don't carry named beneficiaries, such as a house, art, real property, and other personal assets, you can provide instruction on how your assets get distributed through a last will and testament. A will also names the person who is in charge of settling things on your behalf; that person, who used to be called an executor, is now known more commonly as a personal representative. If you have minor children, the will should also include information regarding their care. If they are adults, the document will explain whether and how they will inherit your assets.

3. **Consider a trust.**

   Beneficiary-named assets don't go through probate, the lengthy process where the will must be proven through your personal representative. Everything else does go through probate, in most states, unless you transfer ownership through a revocable living trust, also sometimes known as an *inter vivos* trust. It's a written document, like a will, that lets you transfer your assets to designated beneficiaries according to your specific wishes. A successor trustee helps to distribute the assets after your death. If you do opt for a living trust, you should have a "pour-over will," that includes any assets purchased after the trust was drafted that may have been left out.

4. **Choose a durable power of attorney.**

   To ensure you have someone you can count on to speak on your behalf, name a durable power of attorney to make decisions for you in case you become incapacitated due to injury or illness. The "durable" powers apply to medical and financial issues. Your spouse may or may not have automatic authority, depending on your state.

5. **Get an advance health care directive and name a health care proxy.**

   Also known as a living will, an advance health care directive lets you express your wishes for end-of-life care, including treatment that you don't want. A health care proxy is a person who can make decisions for you about your health. This removes the guesswork for your family should you become incapacitated.

## HAVE YOU ...

- ☐ Reevaluated your budget knowing everything you know now?
- ☐ Considered additional ways to reduce expenses?
- ☐ Checked the veracity of your savings withdrawal rate?
- ☐ Acknowledged and accommodated for potential setbacks?
- ☐ Drafted a will, a durable power of attorney, and an advance health care directive?

### RESOURCES

TheSimpleDollar.com. This website is full of great money-saving ideas and offers a weekly savings roundup that's sent via newsletter.

Caregiver.com checklist for downsizing your home (www.caregiver.org /downsizing-home-checklist-caregivers). Free advice does not get much more in-depth than this very useful checklist for retirees debating whether to stay at home or sell.

*Moving On: A Practical Guide to Downsizing the Family Home* by Linda Hetzer and Janet Hulstrand. Moving is the kind of decision and task that requires serious contemplation. This book has thought of everything and offers practical advice if you do decide to move on.

*The Investor's Manifesto: Preparing for Prosperity, Armageddon, and Everything in Between* by William J. Bernstein. Written by a master of asset allocation and modern portfolio theory, this book will get you thinking about investing risks versus rewards.

*How to Make Your Money Last: The Indispensable Guide* by Jane Bryant Quinn. A new tome from one of my favorite personal finance writers, Quinn focuses on how to make your withdrawal plan work.

Nolo Online Will Software (www.nolo.com/products/online-will-nnwill.html). Ideally, you will have a will drafted by a professional who understands your goals and needs. In the meantime, you need a will ASAP. This software can help. Also check out Nolo's "12 Simple Steps to an Estate Plan" (www.nolo.com/legal-encyclopedia /12-simple-steps-estate-plan-29472.html).

# 3

# BE HAPPIER THAN EVER

I have to confess to my biggest fear: I will work very hard during my career, retire, and be able to do what I love, only to spend all of my free time in retirement playing computer solitaire.

It's a real threat. I always gave my retired mom a hard time for her love of the electronic cards. She is an active volunteer who runs several clubs, participates in everything she can, meets regularly with friends, and helps with the grandkids. She has a pension and Social Security, and she lives frugally. At 65, she got under the sink to fix her own plumbing. Hers is pretty close to the dream retirement. But she seems to have an insatiable weakness for computer solitaire.

For years, I poked fun at my mom for what seemed to be an addiction she had to the game. And then, one day, shortly after I'd left my stressful 9-to-5 job to start my own business, I was networking and looking for new work, but not yet busy, and found myself with nothing to do. Looking for an easy distraction, I picked up my phone and clicked on an ad for mobile solitaire.

I spent hours playing this game. Because the program timed each game and recorded stats for how I performed, I could watch myself progress and get better. That enticed me to keep going, to beat a previous score and in less time.

Wasted hours turned into wasted days. Every morning, I began with the intention to be productive, but the day inevitably became all about mobile solitaire. I started to feel guilt and shame about playing, and worried that it would hurt my chances of having a successful business, but I didn't want to stop. It wasn't until I landed my first serious client that I realized the solitaire needed to go.

Sure, it sounds like a funny story, but when you let go of your daily routine, it's easy to lose focus. There is no end to distractions—from becoming a cable news zealot to getting catfished out of your savings by a stranger on the Internet. Without a plan, it's easy to get bored and anxious or to feel adrift.

# Daily Purpose and a Regular Schedule

Time spent doing what you love or with whom you love. These will help you achieve the goal set out in this third part of the book: be happier than ever. It is achievable, and you are so close.

To lay the groundwork, I want you to run some practice drills. In the next few chapters, we will cover daily routines and work schedules, get you ready for hobbies and travel, check in on your income streams and your budget.

I'm hoping you will save the final chapter to check in a year from now or when your retirement plan goes into action.

## Five Major Milestones

The five steps you will take in this section:

1. Determine how you will spend your time
2. Practice your life in retirement before you retire
3. Prepare for your transition to retirement
4. Retire!
5. Check back in one year on your progress

So let's get started with the truly fun stuff, and prepare to be happier than ever.

# CHAPTER NINE

# Practice Makes Perfect

I'm a big believer that practice and preparation go hand in hand. The more you rehearse something, the better prepared you'll be for show time. This is as true for a professional task as it is for a performance, and it can also be said about your retirement plan. As you prepare for retirement, it helps to practice doing the things you will need to do to succeed.

It may sound counterintuitive, planning so thoroughly for a period in which you will have lots of free time. But as good as free time sounds, it can become as oppressive as work. After a couple of weeks of sleeping late, wasting time on the Internet, and watching too much daytime TV, you'll be looking for something to do. Don't let it be solitaire.

If you need solitaire, sleeping in, and eating ramen noodles in your pjs in front of *Family Feud* reruns, go ahead and build that into your plan, too. Whatever you need to get out of your system, do it—for just a month, if you can stand it.

You might find that you crave structure and need purpose in your everyday life, that you never really liked *Family Feud.* You may be bored and lonely before you've even had a chance to file for Social Security.

# Feather the Breaks

Instead of rushing into retirement life, you can transition gradually over time. Like baby steps, but for seniors. I know you're thinking this is not possible in your case, because you are really, really ready to retire. Maybe so, but it's also possible that you enjoyed your day job more than you thought or tied a great portion of your identity to your work. It's possible that you don't know who you are without sitting behind a nameplate every day. Or you may simply miss the social aspects of work—the greetings, gossip, and good advice that coworkers can provide. Without a plan, you may panic or make poor decisions, sabotaging your own success. If you're married, you may find that you and your spouse are spending too much time together and starting to rub on each other's nerves.

What you need is to prepare for how you will spend your days in retirement. This chapter will help you ease the transition away from work and to support the new decisions you've made. Retiring from your 9-to-5 should not be something that you feel as a system shock—it should be a gradual change that you prepare for, and you should be able to enjoy the transition. Slow down, and get ready.

# Practice Living on a Reduced Income

To know in your head that you live within a new set of means is one thing, to actually live within those means is another. That's why it helps to practice living on your retirement budget a few years (or at least a few months) before you actually retire. Remember how you calculated your estimated monthly Social Security income benefits in chapter 2? Since that's likely to be the bedrock of your guaranteed income in retirement, try to live on that amount or less per month. If you can successfully live on that income, you should have no problem meeting income goals in retirement. Any excess income can be added to savings to boost reserves for the future.

## CREATE A RETIREMENT VISION BOARD

One of my favorite novelists, Dana Spiotta, was interviewed for the *New York Times Magazine* and was described sitting beneath something called a vision board that she'd created for her latest book, *Innocents and Others*.

*". . . she sat beneath a huge bulletin board pinned with her sticky notes and research materials: lists of relevant words (passion, transformation, intimacy) and 'seeing' devices (zoetrope, stereoscope, camera obscura), and photographs of Orson Welles, Jean-Luc Godard, and the Maysles brothers."*

*"'It's like walking into the book,' Spiotta told [the interviewer]. 'You feel it all around you.'"*

How powerful is that? A vision board uses images to tell the story of your goals. Using photo clippings from newspapers, magazines, and personal effects, you can assemble a collage of images that represents the life you want to live in retirement.

It may sound a bit New-Age-meets-Martha-Stewart, but visualization can be a powerful technique for focusing on what you want. Especially if you are a visual thinker, a vision board can represent your retirement goals in a way that's not possible with other types of planning. Even finding and bringing together images and ideas of what you want challenges a different part of your brain and makes your goals seem more immediate. After all, a vision board gives you the means to stare right at them.

Making a vision board is fairly easy. You start with a board, which can be a pin board, canvas, or cork. Pull together favorite images, textures, memorabilia, and inspirational messages: pictures of where you want to be in retirement, what you want to see, feel, experience. Follow your intuition and emotions, rather than what's necessarily in your head. Lay everything out in an arrangement that's appealing to you, and start assembling the board using tape, glue, tacks, or whatever adhesive you have handy. Then view and enjoy.

> Retirement should be like childhood where every day is new and every experience is deeply felt.
>
> JOHN, RETIRED IN THOUSAND OAKS, CALIFORNIA

If the Social Security number doesn't exactly work for you, aim for another amount that limits your spending. For example, try cutting your current monthly budget in half and see how you manage under those restrictions.

Think of it as a game for now, a challenge to find out how you can live if necessary. How thrifty can you be? Can you set a strict limit at a restaurant, a grocery store, on vacation? Living according to a strict budget now will give you a sense of where your budget is vulnerable, and where little luxuries are necessary.

## Practice a Daily Schedule in Retirement

Creating a routine can help you minimize uncertainty and stress in retirement, and help you stay productive and happier. That doesn't mean you have to schedule every minute, but having a set time to wake up, get dressed, eat, and start doing something productive each day is a good idea.

You can even set other daily goals; for example, writing a certain number of words or making a certain number of calls each day. Or you could keep your goals unspecific, for example, setting the goal to do something meaningful each day.

Ultimately it's your schedule, so you can adjust until you find a daily routine that works for you. The point is to create boundaries for yourself that you can live with, and stick to them.

## WORKSHEET 9.1 **YOUR DAILY ROUTINE**

Remember good old Ben Franklin, who helped us supercharge our pros and cons list earlier on in the book? Did I mention he was an early retiree? He began living on passive income from his inventions and businesses at age 42. He was also a big fan of a daily routine. His own, "Daily Scheme," which has been widely shared and is now part of the public domain, is a great template to start with.

| | | |
|---|---|---|
| MORNING QUESTION: WHAT GOOD SHALL I DO THIS DAY? | 5 <br> 6 <br> 7 | RISE, YOGA, WASH AND ADDRESS *POWERFUL GOODNESS*; CONTRIVE DAY'S BUSINESS AND TAKE THE RESOLUTION OF THE DAY; AND BREAKFAST |
| | 8 <br> 9 <br> 10 <br> 11 | WORK |
| | 12 <br> 1 | READ OR OVERLOOK MY ACCOUNTS, AND DINE |
| | 2 <br> 3 <br> 4 | WORK |
| EVENING QUESTION: WHAT GOOD HAVE I DONE TODAY | 5 <br> 6 <br> 7 <br> 8 <br> 9 | PUT THINGS IN THEIR PLACES, SUPPER, MUSIC, OR DIVERSION, OR CONVERSATION; EXAMINATION OF DAY |

➜ There's something so old fashioned, but also cool, about asking yourself what you are going to do this day, and then examining what you've done at the end of the day. I might dedicate one of the four-hour periods before or after lunch to "Fun," and I'd definitely stress inviting friends to the "music, diversion, and conversation" part of the day during mealtimes.

## WHAT WOULD YOUR DAILY ROUTINE LOOK LIKE?

| TIME OF DAY | HOUR | ACTIVITY |
|---|---|---|
| Morning | 5 | |
| | 6 | |
| | 7 | |
| | 8 | |
| | 9 | |
| | 10 | |
| Noon | 11 | |
| | 12 | |
| | 1 | |
| | 2 | |
| | 3 | |
| | 4 | |
| Evening | 5 | |
| | 6 | |
| | 7 | |
| | 8 | |
| | 9 | |
| | 10 | |
| Night | 11 | |
| | 12 | |
| | 1 | |
| | 2 | |
| | 3 | |
| | 4 | |

I do genealogical research on my father's family and spend more time gardening. I spend more time with family in a relaxed setting, lots of three-hour lunches. I have picked grapes at the vineyard and made grape wine from scratch, as well as from other fresh fruits. I spent part of every day with my mother during the last six months of her life.

LETTIE, RETIRED IN LANCASTER, PENNSYLVANIA

## Practice a Move to a New Place

If you plan on making a move in retirement and you've been considering a new city, state, or country, use some of your vacation time to spend a week or two in your destination to get to know the place. Before purchasing a home in any new location, it makes sense to rent first and get a feel for the area before you commit.

This is where services like Airbnb really come in handy. If you can, find one or two short-term rentals in your dream destination, to get a feel for neighborhood life outside of the tourist zones. Ask yourself: Could I be happy living here? Are there activities that interest me? People with whom I could be friends? How is the weather?

## Practice Your Hobby Every Day

Remember the list of things that make you truly happy from chapter 1? What will it take to make some of those things a part of your daily life? If it's reaching out to others to make plans with the people you love, then start making the connections. If it's a hobby or activity, create the space and resources to make those things work. If you're planning to sew, fire up the sewing machine, find the fabrics, and get the patterns out. If you plan to build furniture, sharpen the tools. And if you plan to sit at a desk, create a space that's conducive to work.

# Practice Being Together All of the Time

If you think it's going to be bliss retiring at the same time as your spouse, you might also prepare yourself for an alternate reality: one where the two of you can't seem to get in sync, don't want to do the same things at the same time (if at all), and may eventually want to run screaming back to your respective jobs.

It's not easy to retire on someone else's schedule, but it's something that married couples may have to face. Mitzie, a retiree in Kansas City, was thrilled to be able to retire within months of her husband; the couple couldn't wait to be able to enjoy more free time together. When retirement came, she realized that she and her husband had very different ideas about how they should spend their time. While she preferred reading and relaxing, he was restless and needed to take on projects around the house.

All that togetherness? It wasn't exactly what Mitzie expected, either. She and her husband spent a lot of time bumping into one another and getting on each other's nerves.

Eventually, Mitzie realized that she and her husband actually needed regular time away from each other. Once she found volunteer projects to keep her busy and out of the house, she was better prepared to spend more quality time at home with her spouse the rest of the time.

Even if you've discussed retirement plans with your spouse, share some of the exercises in this book to help him or her get a better sense of your retirement vision. Plan your daily schedules together, so there are no illusions about what each of you wants in retirement. Better yet—ask your spouse to do some of the exercises, too!

> I have found that I am perfectly happy doing nothing, while my husband is compelled to do stuff all the time. He recently confided that he has promised himself that he will do something that matters every day. On the days that I am tired, I can just relax, read a book, or watch a movie. Some days, I am quite busy with housework, laundry, and grocery shopping.
>
> MICHELE, RETIRED IN WINNETKA, CALIFORNIA

# The Keys to Happiness

Here are suggestions for what to do with your free time to make you feel happy and relaxed.

## VOLUNTEERING

Volunteering has been scientifically found to combat stress and help improve mental health. No wonder more than 30 million people age 55 or older volunteered in 2014,[60] according to the Bureau of Labor Statistics.

The government study found that volunteerism tapers off with age. But in the early years of retirement, volunteering offers a way to stay active in the community, to stay connected to younger generations, and to continue to do meaningful work.

## EXERCISE

Another activity that falls under the category of "better late than never" is regular exercise. Exercise has been found to help with depression, memory loss, even Alzheimer's and Parkinson's diseases.[61] Plus when you exercise, your brain releases endorphins, which make you happy. Even among people who've never worked out in their lives, exercise can lead to dramatic improvements in health and well-being. One British study looked at people who had taken up physical activity at age 63 or older and watched them for eight years. They found that becoming and remaining active at that age could help with healthy aging.[62]

There is growing support for seniors looking to stay active, including new "senior playgrounds," which have been gaining popularity around the globe and have recently started arriving in US cities. Like children's playgrounds, these are free spaces with equipment designed to get you climbing, stepping, spinning, and sliding, if a little more gingerly than you did as a kid. What could be better for inciting happiness?

With a bit of research, you may be able to find free fitness classes in your area. Meetup is a great resource for free events and trial opportunities at local gyms and workout studios. You can also head to YouTube and watch workout videos for free. If you are enrolled in Medicare, you can take part in one of hundreds of Silver Sneakers fitness classes across the country—you may even have access to it through your pre-retirement health plan. Better yet, find a friend who is ready to get moving, and build regular walks or hikes into your daily or weekly routine.

## ACTIVITIES RANGING IN INTENSITY

### Low Intensity

- Low-impact strength or resistance work
- Gardening
- Walking, 3 miles an hour or less
- Water aerobics
- Yoga

### Moderate Intensity

- Biking
- Brisk walking, 3 miles an hour or faster
- Swimming
- Tennis (doubles)

### High Intensity

- Aerobics routine
- Combination cardio and strength or resistance work
- Hiking
- Jogging
- Tennis (singles)

> I take great care of my health. I exercise a lot. I go to Pilates three days a week. (I deduct it as a medical expense from my HSA.) I walk and ride my bike. I cook my own food. I socialize and I help my daughter and her husband. I sleep late, read a lot, and do needlework. And I still work. I need more money to travel.
>
> MARY, RETIRED IN PROVIDENCE, RHODE ISLAND

## Brain Games

Just as it's important to keep the rest of your body physically healthy and active, your brain needs a workout routine, too. Good nutrition and cardiovascular exercise help, but the brain needs to be constantly challenged to stay active.

The Internet has tried to respond to this need by offering online brain games (for a fee) designed to improve cognitive health. A number of studies by neurologists have measured the effectiveness of these games and found that they did little to enhance cognition in older adults.[63] You might get better at the specific skills the game requires, but that skill does not necessarily transfer to lasting improvements in memory or problem-solving.[64]

Turns out, your brain works better on the job or in real-life situations. Learning something new, such as a language, game, or instrument, can help keep you mentally sharp. Drawing something from recall, such as a map or layout, or memorizing something you need to recall, such as a shopping list, can also help stimulate your brain. If you are going to use puzzles, free crossword puzzles and Sudoku puzzles can be highly effective, as can reading parts of the paper you hadn't looked at previously. In general, exposing yourself to new experiences and learning new things is most effective for keeping your brain sharp.

# Travel

Remember that study about how experiences make you happier than material possessions? That idea seems like an endorsement for travel, which for many people is longed-for retirement reward. Whether you have dreamed of hitting the road in a Winnebago, trotting across the globe, or just spending a lot more time near the grandkids, travel can be a great way to spend your time, if you keep it on the cheap. Here are some ideas.

1. **Start with a budget.**

   Your retirement income should be so regimented as to make it easy to come up with a number allotted for discretionary travel. If you don't have room in your budget this year, it can be a goal to work toward in the future.

2. **Don't rely on Internet sites.**

   The hospitality industry has caught up with Internet efficiencies, making travel deals a lot harder to find. Sites like Expedia, Travelocity, Kayak, and others are still fine resources for checking out comparable prices, but it pays to head straight to the site of your preferred airline and check rates directly from the source. And, talk about retro, travel agents have started popping up to help people make the best, most cost-effective decisions.

3. **Use your senior status.**

   Remember, retirement is not the time to be shy about asking for a senior discount. Mention it when booking travel, and you may be able to knock up to 10 percent off quoted rates. Or look for deals on senior cruises or through senior tour groups, where the agent takes advantage of every discount and passes the savings along to you.

> The first thing I wanted to do when I retired was fundamentally change my diet and start exercising to improve my health so I can enjoy the rest of my life. I never had the time before, or thought I didn't. Exercising every day and making major diet changes, I lost over 31 pounds and gained physical improvements across the board.
>
> SCOTT, RETIRED IN ANN ARBOR, MICHIGAN

4. **House swap or house sit.**

While it may sound shady, the Internet has made it easier than ever to trade homes with people who live in great spots and want to vacation where you are. Sites like HomeExchange or HomeAway can help you book a property and vet people interested in booking yours. Or if you are looking for longer-term places to stay, TrustedHousesitters is a great place to find free board in exchange for housesitting, pet sitting, and plant watering.

5. **Try voluntourism.**

A volunteer vacation is a great way to travel on the cheap, see the world in a new way, and help a cause that's worthy to you. The number of volunteer opportunities around the country and the world continues to grow. Look at VolunteerMatch.org, Projects-Abroad.org, and REI for opportunities. If you have your own RV, a group called NOMADS (Nomads on a Mission Active in Divine Service, nomadsumc.org/) works with the United Methodist Church to bring volunteers where they are needed for outreach and disaster rebuilding.

# Love

If you're part of a couple, build time into your schedule for your spouse or significant other. Make sure to plan time to do activities of your own, too. When a couple retire together, it can be too much of a good thing.

If you're unmarried, you may have the opposite problem, looking for love in retirement. While this is not a dating book, I have promised to tackle the subject of happiness, and finding love is part of that. Here are a few tips:

- **Stay engaged with the outside world.** The first step for meeting someone new is to be around new people. It's even better to be around new people who you have things in common with, which is why it's so important to remain connected to information and events in the community.

- **Keep an open mind.** The Internet makes it easier to meet someone from the comfort of your own keyboard, and people ages 60 and older represent one of the fastest-growing demographics in online dating.[65] Stay away from "hookup" sites like Tinder and favor profile-matching sites like eHarmony, Match's Our Time, SeniorPeopleMeet, Dating.AARP, and more.

- **Go with who you know.** In the end, you may have better luck finding a connection within your existing social networks, such as Facebook, Instagram, Twitter, Vine, and LinkedIn. You never know when you'll reconnect with a lost love or missed connection worthy of do over.

- **Trust your friends.** Have friends or colleagues recommend and introduce you to new folks, or stick with a dating site that can vet some of the worst-case weirdos.

I do a lot. My husband and I usually go out 3 or 4 nights a week to dinners with friends, concerts, meetings, etc. I always loved to swim and now it's part of my life again. In the summer, I swim in the lakes and in the winter, I swim at the college pools. We take the dogs on long walks every day. I belong to a book group, a casual lunch group, and a group of women who canoe in the summer and ski in the winter. I am much more physically active, and it makes me happy to see that my strength and my skills are improving. I also do a lot of volunteer work, but I am trying to cut back because it takes so much time and because it reminds me too much of working—all the drama, none of the money. I have been teaching myself the craft of shibori (a Japanese method of dyeing fabric), and I will be teaching a class on it. My husband and I also travel.

SUSAN, RETIRED IN SARANAC LAKE, NEW YORK

## WORKSHEET 9.2 **YOUR SOCIAL CALENDAR**

| THINGS TO DO | TIME COMMITMENT |
|---|---|
| | _____ hours per week/month |
| | _____ hours per week/month |
| | _____ hours per week/month |
| | _____ hours per week/month |
| | _____ hours per week/month |
| | _____ hours per week/month |
| | _____ hours per week/month |

The first time I ever heard of mah jongg, it was in a punchline of a Woody Allen joke about how after he was expelled from NYU, his mother went into the bathroom and took an overdose of mah jongg tiles.

The next time I heard about mah jongg was when my own mother, who is probably a good 15 years younger than Allen himself, joined a group of retired women who meet and play the ancient Chinese game every Friday. She enjoys it so much that my brother gifted her with some antique tiles. Mah jongg may not be the key to happiness, but it's something she really loves to do in retirement.

These days it's hard to find a retiree . . . okay, maybe it's hard to find a retired woman who isn't playing mah jongg. The rummy-like game, played with intricate tiles instead of cards, first came to America in the 1920s, when a businessman named Joseph P. Babcock brought the game from China and started marketing sets. It grew in popularity, particularly among women in Jewish communities during and after World War II. It was all the rage in Catskill's summer bungalows in the 1950s and 1960s.[66] (This is probably when Woody's mom would have played.)

Perhaps it was those same women who helped keep the game popular among retirees a half-century later? I'm not sure, but it seems it's easy to pick up a mah jongg game through a local group or senior center. You can also check out the National Mah Jongg League at nationalmahjonggleague.org/.

## WORKSHEET 9.3 **YOUR ACTIVITY BUDGET**

Let's go back to the latest version of your budget, but isolate only the items related to entertainment and activity. Considering some of the activities discussed in this chapter, do items need to be added to this budget, and do estimated expenses need to be adjusted?

| ACTIVITY | EXPENSES |
|---|---|
| Dining out | $ _____ × _____ per week = $ _____ |
| Entertaining | $ _____ × _____ per week = $ _____ |
| Hobbies | $ _____ × _____ per week = $ _____ |
| Entertainment | $ _____ × _____ per week = $ _____ |
| Classes | $ _____ × _____ per week = $ _____ |
| Vacations/travel | $ _____ × _____ per week = $ _____ |
| Exercise | $ _____ × _____ per week = $ _____ |
| Other | $ _____ × _____ per week = $ _____ |
| Other | $ _____ × _____ per week = $ _____ |
| Other | $ _____ × _____ per week = $ _____ |
| Other | $ _____ × _____ per week = $ _____ |
| Other | $ _____ × _____ per week = $ _____ |

➜ Discretionary total $ _____ × 12 months = $ _____ per year

## HAVE YOU . . .

- ☐ Practiced being retired?
- ☐ Created a daily and weekly schedule that incorporates hobbies and activities you enjoy?
- ☐ Developed a retirement vision board?
- ☐ Tried living on a budget?
- ☐ Shared your retirement vision with your spouse? Discussed what married life will be like in retirement?
- ☐ Determined your budget for entertainment and activities?

### RESOURCES

Go4Life (go4life.nia.nih.gov/). The National Institute on Aging's exercise site offers featured daily exercises, lets you keep track of your progress, and keeps you informed and inspired with stories of how other seniors got fit.

Corporation for National & Community Service (www.nationalservice.gov/programs /senior-corps). This site connects individuals age 55 and older with volunteer opportunities that need them, including foster grandparent volunteer roles.

National Mah Jongg League (www.nationalmahjonggleague.org/). This group was formed in 1937 by enthusiasts who wanted to standardize the game, and today it still exists to publish the official, modern American version of the rules, sell merchandise, answer questions, and help you find games in your area.

Trusted Housesitters (trustedhousesitters.com). A great site if you are looking for a house or pet sitter you can trust at no cost. It's also a place to look for cool housesitting gigs that allow you to stay for free in locations around the world—for a weekend, a few weeks, or even a season. There is a monthly membership fee of $8.25, but you can access the site for free to learn more, chat with an expert, and get started.

"The Reason Vision Boards Work and How to Make One" (www.huffingtonpost.com /elizabeth-rider/the-scientific-reason-why_b_6392274.html). Learn how to create visual goals from wellness expert Elizabeth Rider.

*Benjamin Franklin: An American Life* by Walter Isaacson. This book is a definitive biography of a true retirement hero.

Creative Routines of Famous People (https://podio.com/site/creative-routines). Looking for inspiration? Check out this site that posts the daily rituals of the most creative artists of all time.

CHAPTER

# TEN

# Get Ready for Go Time

I'm useless at any sport aside from tennis, so I'll forgo referring to the period right before you retire as an important stretch, down, inning, or even set point. Those analogies may work for some people, but they do little to convey the frantic intensity of preparing right up to the very last moment. The only analogy I can think of comes from *Project Runway*, the TV show. Imagine you are one of the designers on *Project Runway* and this is the 10 minutes before Tim will insist that you get to the runway. You know, the 10 minutes when everyone frantically sews, staples, or glues their models into their gowns before time is up? The period right before retirement is like those 10 minutes.

What's involved in these final 10 minutes will be checking to make sure your plan is in place and making small changes and fixes that may impact the final outcome. It's time to deal with your own emotions, fears, and nerves, and mentally prepare for what's to come. Most important, it's time to assess what you've done and feel a sense of accomplishment. Congratulations on reaching this point in life!

**Y**ou may or may not encounter problems in your plan, but to ease your mind I've included throughout this chapter some contingency plans for very specific things that could go wrong.

Unfortunately, I can't think of everything. Everyone's circumstances are different—and the problems as well as the solutions will vary. You may find that one or more of these situations apply to you. The advice included in this chapter is designed to help you prioritize your thinking in any circumstance and conquer the most common problems. Nothing is going to come easily, but with a bit of planning you can get over retirement stumbling blocks.

There's also a sense of calm that comes with knowing that a plan is in place and you are ready to execute it. Enjoy that, as well. You've earned the right to feel confident, you deserve to succeed, and there's no problem that you haven't prepared for. Did I mention that staying positive, optimistic, and grateful are also important aspects of a successful retirement plan?

# Let Everyone Know

Now that your plan is set, it's time to think about sharing it with others. There's no specific rule for how much advance notice to give when you plan to retire, but the following timeline can give you a sense of how you might announce your impending retirement.

## WHEN TO ANNOUNCE WHAT AND TO WHOM

Timing is everything, as the saying goes. You want to be the one to break the news about this important transition in your life. I've assembled a timeline that begins roughly a year before you actually

If you follow a disciplined, sustainable portfolio withdrawal plan like those outlined in chapter 2, you should not run out of investment savings. Even in the event of a market crash, your portfolio should still sustain your withdrawals and be able to bounce back over time. That said, you could pull out too much each year, or make the wrong investments, and end up depleting your savings earlier than expected.

### WHAT'S THE PLAN B?

The only ways to compensate are by working more or further reducing your spending. Define exactly how much you need to bring in to make up for what was lost in your portfolio. It may only be an extra $200 per week or $1000 per month, which you may be able to make up for by reducing your spending, for example through less expensive housing options, downsizing from two cars to one, or cooking exclusively at home. Try different online tools to help you track spending and keep overhead low.

You can also make up for the savings gap by taking on additional work hours, raising the price you charge for your work, and finding additional income sources. This is the time to get creative (and not just on Etsy, although that's a good place to sell any crafts you might make). Consider taking odd jobs on TaskRabbit or Craigslist, or selling items you no longer use on eBay.

If you do go back to work, rebuild your savings with dividend-paying investments, which can help you begin to generate income to cover future expenses. To avoid this problem in the future, periodically reevaluate whether your withdrawal strategy still makes sense.

retire. Use it as a guideline. Your timeline may differ, of course. For example, some of you may want to talk over the retirement decision with your spouse first of all.

- **10–12 months from retirement: Spouse and Close Family**
  After learning more about retirement options through your human resources department, it makes sense to speak to a spouse, significant other, or children about your retirement plans in the near future. Family and very close friends can help support and advise you through the transition, and may be able to help you anticipate issues before they happen.

- **10–12 months from retirement: Human Resources** If you have at least a year until retirement, contact your human resources department around 10 to 12 months from your planned date. The HR representative can help you understand important steps or deadlines to meet before retirement. And if you are looking for flexible work options, human resources is the right place to turn.

- **6 months from retirement: Your Boss** At about six months out, it makes sense to confirm the date with your direct manager. This may not be easy if the department relies on you. You can leave the timing open to negotiation, based on the employer's needs—you may even get some freelance work as a parting gift.

- **1–6 months from retirement: Your Coworkers** Once you have a set date, find a way to let people that you work with know the news. The last thing you want is to be caught up in suspicion and gossip, and everyone will be relieved to hear the news coming from you.

- **1 month from retirement: Your Professional Networks**
  Head to LinkedIn, Facebook, and any other network where friends and professional contacts may intersect. Post a brief note announcing your retirement, and your plans for what's next. Again, if you are looking for new work (and maybe even if you're not), this is a great time to introduce yourself as a newly marketable entity.

- **1 week from retirement: Colleagues Throughout Your Company** Before you leave the job, send a departing note to colleagues in your department. If your company has fewer than 100 employees, you might consider sending an email note to everyone in the company, or just everyone in your department, depending on protocol within your firm. Similarly, if you are particularly close with coworkers in your department, personal handwritten notes can add a special touch.

# Retirement Checklist

Before you finish the book and cross the finish line into retirement, let's make sure to cross off the following items from your list. Now is the time to tackle anything that's left undone. You don't have to implement each item at the same time. Some may need to be taken care of immediately and others can wait. For example, early on you will probably want to make the decision about when to claim Social Security, but you may not yet know when you are going to move. Still other items, such as your withdrawal strategy, will need to be adjusted from time to time. The main thing, though, is that you have given each item on the list considerable thought and made your decisions accordingly.

## INCOME

- ☐ Do you know where your income is coming from for the first 6 to 12 months in retirement?
- ☐ Do you need to increase savings?
- ☐ Does your withdrawal strategy still make sense?
- ☐ Have you made a decision about when to claim Social Security?
- ☐ How is your progress in terms of new income streams? Do you need to add income?

**B**ecause this plan involves doing some work in retirement, finding a job (at least one) is an important factor in your success. Anyone who has looked for employment over the age of 40 knows how daunting it can be to find a job that you want or that wants you. When the overall economy is bad, it can be downright painful.

### WHAT'S THE PLAN B?

The first step is to adjust your thinking. While it may be true that fewer companies are willing to consider you now than would have 20 years ago, unemployment for those age 55 or older is lower than the overall rate for the total population, age discrimination cases are down, and more companies are creating employment retraining programs for senior workers. Companies who have a reputation for hiring older workers include Deloitte, CVS, Barclay's, National Institutes of Health, Stanley Consultants, MetLife, McKinsey, and many others.

Instead of feeling desperate, broaden the scope of what you can do to bring in income. Talk to your friends, family members, and former colleagues. Consider everything from marketing to life coaching, from housesitting to babysitting, from handiwork to homework help, from temping to training others. If you expand your horizons, you will find money-making opportunities.

If you would prefer to work for a large organization, do some research to find companies that favor older workers. The AARP used to create an annual list, but no longer updates it. In general, the types of companies included on the list were universities, health organizations, credit unions, and government organizations.

Networking is still one of the surest ways to find opportunities. Jobs at your level may not be advertised, and when a company wants someone who is available for a short-term project, you want your name to be on their minds. Keep open communication with your professional networks through sites like LinkedIn.com, join professional organizations, and mentor or offer advice to colleagues (through social media, blogs, and continuing education courses). Most important, stay in touch with friends and colleagues in your field who may know of opportunities.

## BUDGET

☐ Do you have a plan to pay off any debt?

☐ Do you need to make additional cuts?

☐ Have you refined your budget from chapter 4? Do you have a budget you can stick to? (Have you practiced sticking to it?)

## SAVING

☐ Do you have a plan to continue saving in retirement?

☐ Do you have plans to rebalance on a regular schedule (once every one to two years, unless markets shift dramatically)?

☐ Do you have six to nine months' worth of savings for emergencies? Have you continued to add to your savings as you plan and prepare for retirement?

☐ Have you increased your 401(k) contribution amount for the year? Could you attempt to contribute the maximum in the year or years before you leave your job?

☐ Is your asset allocation in line with your goals and risk tolerance?

## ESTATE PLANNING

☐ Do you have a durable power of attorney and advance medical directive?

☐ Have you checked your beneficiaries?

☐ Have you created a will? Does the executor and/or beneficiary know where the will is located?

## INSURANCE

☐ Are you covered by disability insurance?

☐ Do you have your calendar marked to file for Medicare at age 65?

☐ Do you understand your Medicare options and how each part works?

**B**eneficiaries are the individuals who will receive financial benefits from your accounts when you die. You can list more than one beneficiary, as a way to divide the money; for example, one third of your IRA can be inherited by each of your three children. You may also list more than one beneficiary as a way to provide a line of succession to the funds; for example, your spouse is the first beneficiary, and if he or she is no longer alive when you die, your nephew is next in line to become the beneficiary.

Are the correctly named beneficiaries listed on your financial accounts? If you have a will or estate plan, your beneficiaries should have been mapped out. Consistency counts, or else you risk voiding the will. For example, it makes more sense to divide each account equally instead of leaving one account to one heir and another account to a different heir. Better yet, let the assets pass into a trust (trusts and charities can also be named beneficiaries), and have the trust divide up the assets according to your wishes. If you want your assets to become part of a trust, you will have to pay a lawyer to set it up. There is no fee to simply list the beneficiary or beneficiaries you have chosen to inherit specific accounts. Their names should be part of your routine paperwork.

## COMMON BENEFICIARY-NAMED ACCOUNTS

- Annuity
- Brokerage account
- Checking account
- Insurance policy
- IRA
- Roth IRA

- 401(k)
- 403(b)
- Other IRA (SEP)
- Money market account
- Savings bonds
- Savings account

One or more of the scenarios in this chapter could put you in a situation where you decide to or are forced to "un-retire" and go back to work full-time.

### WHAT'S THE PLAN B?

If you must go back to work for someone else, try to do it on your terms, either by training for something new or working in a job that is more suited to you. The website irelaunch.com can help you find companies that specifically retrain older workers. You can also look for jobs that offer telecommuting or flexible hours to retain some sense of independence.

☐ Have you planned for health coverage in retirement?

☐ Have you contributed to a tax-deferred Health Savings Account?

☐ Have you investigated long-term care insurance options?

## HOME

☐ Are you going to downsize, move, or stay in your home?

☐ Do you know where you will live in retirement?

☐ If you plan to move, have you researched the new area and spent time there?

☐ If you plan to stay, can you pay off your mortgage or find other ways to reduce monthly housing costs?

## HOBBIES

☐ Can you make money doing one or more of your hobbies?

☐ Do you know what you love to do most?

☐ Do you want to do that thing you love most in retirement?

E ven if you are set financially, you may hate retirement for other reasons.

## WHAT'S THE PLAN B?

Go back to school. More than 150,000 people in the United States participate in the Osher Lifelong Learning Institutes, funded through the Bernard Osher Foundation, which are programs affiliated with national colleges and universities that allow seniors to sit in on classes for free. Your local college or university may do something similar, to encourage seniors to get involved. Learning is great for keeping the brain stimulated, and it offers a way to expand your horizons while staying close to home. But the best part is the opportunities to socialize on a campus setting.

Going back to school may also help re-energize your creative spirit and put you in the mood to produce income doing something new and interesting.

If you're really not interested in school or don't have a program near you, you can still follow the learning theme and participate in local classes or programs in your community. The library is often a good place to start, and these days you can just as easily find postings and event calendars online. Plenty of organizations cater to senior events, but anything free in the community is probably worth exploring.

- ☐ Have you decided which hobbies will occupy your time?
- ☐ Have you stocked up on supplies necessary to make the most of your hobby?

## SOCIAL LIFE

- ☐ Have you reached out to friends and family via handwritten notes, email, or social networks?
- ☐ Have you shared your retirement vision and retirement plans with your spouse?
- ☐ Have you told your family you plan to retire?

# The Happiness Checklist

I've separated this checklist because even after you've marked off the items, this work must be done on an ongoing basis. Check in with this list often.

- ☐ **Have you adjusted your attitude?** For this plan to work you must believe that you deserve to retire and it can happen for you.

- ☐ **Are you staying optimistic?** Have the confidence that you can generate income for yourself in retirement and enjoy yourself more. Remind yourself of future you, the one who comes back to tell you how amazing retirement is.

- ☐ **Do you count yourself grateful?** Remind yourself of all that you have accomplished, the valuable skills you have to offer, support from family and friends, and anything else for which you can be grateful.

- ☐ **Do you take time to enjoy the little things?** Revisit the list of things that are the most meaningful to you. Are you finding time to think about those on a regular basis?

- ☐ **Are you giving back?** Find ways to be kind, to help others, and to participate in charity. These endeavors help you see beyond your own problems to give something back to the world.

**F**alling on bad health is bad for any retirement plan, but it could mean disaster for a plan that requires you to work part of the time.

## WHAT'S THE PLAN B?

You can prepare for bad health by having safeguards in place. Having disability insurance can help protect a portion of your income in the event of illness or injury. Health insurance will cover a portion of your expenses, and once you reach age 65, Medicare will take over your insurance coverage, and the premiums are low.

If your health problems are extreme, Medicare does not cover long-term care insurance, but Medicaid does for those who qualify.

While you are working, saving extra income in a Health Savings Account (HSA), for those who have access to one, can help you cover future expenses through tax-free investment earnings. To be in an HSA, you must be enrolled in a high-deductible health plan, which does not make sense for everyone. But if you already have an HSA, make the most of it. You can also save extra dollars in a Roth IRA and achieve a similar goal.

You should also have your durable power of attorney, advance health care directive, and health care proxy in place so that you know your interests will be taken care of in the future. It should go without saying that maintaining healthful habits should be a part of Plan A as well as Plan B.

If you are in poor health, it makes sense to take Social Security as soon as you are able and to consider your withdrawal strategy factoring in a new longevity outlook. As depressing as it sounds, you want to use your money efficiently while you are alive. You also have to consider what will happen to your spouse and his or her plan once you are not.

> When people are in the process of retiring, they seem to panic about what to do with their time. I tell them not to worry. Relax. They will find things to do. We live in a wonderful time to be old. Good health care, medications, good doctors, tons of things to do, and fantastic senior groups. It is truly the golden years. And, if you are really lucky, grandkids. The most important thing to do is to keep moving!
>
> DEENA, RETIRED IN BEND, OREGON

## The Big Moment

I keep thinking back to a quote from the writer Goethe that a friend shared with me as I began writing this book: "Whatever you can do, or dream you can, begin it." It reminds me of the importance of taking a leap, of attempting what you can or dream you can do, instead of putting it off and never knowing what's possible.

If you have done the work in this book, you should be prepared to do the thing you have dreamed of, to begin the next chapter of your life. This is the calm before the fun begins, and you've earned it, so take this moment to enjoy it.

This is the last chapter for now. I'd like you to come back to the book and read the final chapter, Focus on Happiness, one year into retirement. It will help you track your progress and see how far you've come, and tackle any problems that may have come up in your first year as a retiree.

For now, smile, put your feet up, gloat a little bit. You defied the odds and are ready to retire. You have the tools you need to succeed and even surpass your expectations for what is possible.

You're a total badass!

## HAVE YOU . . .

- ☐ Developed a timeline for announcing your retirement to human resources, your manager and coworkers, and your social networks?

- ☐ Gone through the retirement checklist to make sure everything is covered?

- ☐ Considered the happiness checklist and the ongoing work that needs to be done there?

### RESOURCES

Making the Transition: A Pre-Retirement Checklist (www.401khelpcenter.com /401k_education/retirement_checklist.html). The 401(k) Help Center provides a timeline of what to do in the buildup to retirement.

How to Write a Goodbye Email to Your Coworkers (www.huffingtonpost.com /sarah-cooper/how-to-write-a-goodbye-em_b_7843358.html). A detailed look into the perfect way to say goodbye via email.

Bankrate Retirement Calculators (www.bankrate.com/calculators/index-of-retirement -calculators.aspx?ic_id=calc-lead_retirement_retirement_globalnav). If you need to run some last-minute numbers, Bankrate's a great place to find easy-to-use calculators.

# CHAPTER
# ELEVEN

# Focus on Happiness

Welcome back! If you are reading this chapter you have embarked on a retirement that once seemed impossible. (Or you were too impatient to wait for an entire year after finishing everything else in the book; in which case, check back one year after retirement.) Congratulations on putting in the hard work to make retirement happen. I'm sure that you have learned a few things along the way.

This final chapter is designed to help you check in, to make sure that the plan you started with still makes sense. You should feel confident that you can continue to live comfortably in retirement, and that your plan has the power to last. And you should still be focused on the goal you started with in this book: happiness.

Are you practicing mindful happiness each day? Focusing on the things and people you enjoy most? Have you found a more flexible and more fulfilling way to earn income?

# How Are Your Income Streams?

Is your plan to generate enough income in retirement still an effective one? If your hobby business turned out to be a chore, or your part-time fun job isn't nearly as fun as you thought it would be, you can make adjustments to your income plan. Revisit chapters 6 and 7 to get ideas for additional ways to bring in potential income.

On the other hand, your problem may be that business is booming to the point that you can't keep up. Scaling up a business that's based on services that only you can provide is a real challenge. The risk is that you work more hours to keep up with demand and burn out on something that you once enjoyed.

There are things you can do. You can delegate work to others you know and trust, perhaps other retirees with the same plan in mind. You can outsource some of your administration and billing. There are plenty of virtual assistance companies you can find online who are willing to lend a hand at a reasonable price. You could find tools or develop systems that help you increase efficiency and save time. Or you could find a way to turn your service into a product that is able to reach a lot more people without adding further strain to your resources.

# How Is Your Budget?

Home upkeep, unforeseen family expenses, or even a hobby that costs more than you had anticipated are just a few of the things that can blow up your budget.

If you get off track and have to withdraw more than you expected from your savings in a given year, snap right back into place for the next year. Short-term blips are to be expected, but staying with your long-term plan still matters. If you need help, try another spending diary where you track expenses for one month. Where have expenses gone off track?

If you are relying too much on credit, find a way to reduce your usage—at least for impulse buys. Try to purchase things with cash when you can. And negotiate with creditors to lower your interest rate while you can.

Don't be afraid of the future, there are so many unexpected surprises and mysteries that will be revealed.

ALICE, RETIRED IN SARASOTA, FLORIDA

# How Is Your Savings Plan?

Have you continued to add to your savings in retirement? Do you feel more or less financially stable than you did a year ago?

How about your investment portfolio? Your investment balance will grow more slowly in retirement and may even decrease during periods of poor market performance. This may make it more difficult for you to remain invested and stick with your long-term investment plan.

Remember that moving your assets when the market is behaving badly is akin to market timing—and it usually ends up badly. The market goes up and down, but gains tend to come in concentrated periods. Data from investment behemoth Fidelity found that investors tend to increase their allocations to stocks ahead of downturns (i.e., buying into the hottest, "can't miss" stocks) and decrease their allocations to stocks just before market gains (i.e., running from stocks when nobody else seems to want them). Clearly, your investments will gain if you do the opposite. Buy low and sell high is the way to go.

The problem with pulling your money out of the market is that if you miss a day, week, or month of significant gains, it could severely hinder the long-term growth of your portfolio.

Take a look at the hypothetical growth of $10,000 invested in the Standard & Poor's 500 Index from January 1, 1980, to March 31, 2015. The tallest column, on the far left, represents the high earnings of an investor who left his or her money in the stock market for 35 years. The shortest column, on the far right, represents the much smaller earnings of an investor who pulled his money at such times to miss the best 50 earnings days in those 35 years. The problem is that it's

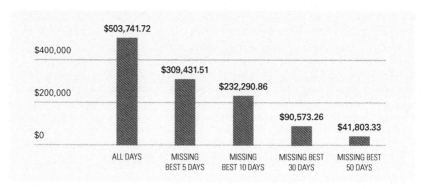

Source: Fidelity Investments https://www.fidelity.com/viewpoints/investing-ideas /strategies-for-volatile-markets

impossible for anyone up to foresee when those "best days" will occur. The lesson is that staying in for the long haul, regardless of market volatility, is the tried-and-true strategy to increase your savings.[67]

When markets are volatile, regular investors can benefit from them. Think of a bear market like you would a sale: if there's something worth buying, you can get it on the cheap.

# How's the Happiness?

Joy in retirement may be harder to measure than other factors, but you know it when you feel it. If things have gone relatively easy during the first year of retirement, you are likely to be content. But have you taken the extra step of practicing those things that you most enjoy? If not, it's time to revisit your list and designate some time for a hobby. Trust me, it's good for you.

If you're not feeling happy, there may be many reasons. If you had a difficult time breaking from your day job and coworkers, it could put you in a funk. Or maybe you spend too much or not enough time with the people closest to you. You may be having an existential crisis, or you may miss going out to dinner and a movie once in a while. Make the adjustments you think will improve your happiness, and give it more time. And remember it's okay to take the time you need to adjust to this enormous life change. Some people find transitioning to change harder than others.

You do learn that you can live on less and still have a good life.

WILLA, RETIRED IN CHARLOTTESVILLE, VIRGINIA

# Planning for Different Stages in Retirement

Now that you've reached retirement, there's something you should know: you could live through more than one phase of retirement. There may be up to three stages to go through during your post-working years:

1. **Early retirement.**

   This is the period when you continue to do some work, actively engage in hobbies, travel, and adventure. You will likely spend more in this period on discretionary activities and entertainment. Most of this book has focused on early retirement.

2. **Middle retirement.**

   This is when your retirement has matured into more of a routine, you stick closer to home, and most adventure comes from regular social activities or spending time with friends and family. While you may continue to bring in income, your work should taper off dramatically during this period, and your plan may need to adapt to fit your circumstances. At some point, you will probably no longer be able to enjoy work. If you have continued to save and follow the withdrawal strategy established before retirement, this should be feasible, but it may require adjustments to your expenses and budget. Because health issues may become more of a concern during this period, rest and relaxation are a priority. You may devote more of your budget to medical bills during this stage.

3. **Late retirement.**

   This is when your activities may be limited by what your body allows. You may not have the physical health to be as active and mobile as you once were. Of course, you may also be the forever young and spry exception, but you will not likely spend as much during this period on entertainment, travel, or even hobbies. If you had been living an adventure in some far-flung place, you may want to move closer to loved ones who can help support you in your advanced age. A retirement community, senior living facility, or nursing home may be a next step as you advance in age and encounter health and mobility issues that keep you from living an independent life. Long-term care and general medical expenses will likely be your biggest expense, and you may need to rely on outside services to help meet expenses.

# Caregiving in Retirement

When I asked retirees what worried them, the answer I heard most often was a resounding, "Health!" Yet what is more likely to derail an individual's retirement plan was not his or her illness, but taking care of someone else in ailing health.

More than 43.5 million Americans act as informal or family caregivers to an adult who is ill, disabled, or aged, according to the AARP.[68] Offering to care for someone you love is the kind of thing you do without being asked, without even thinking about it. But it can take up a good deal of your time, energy, and financial and emotional resources—all of which can become spare in retirement.

Caregiving can be distracting, tiring, and emotionally draining. Unfortunately, it can also drain your resources, not only money, but also your time to take on other projects, to bring in retirement income, and to do what you enjoy. If you are struggling, don't be afraid to ask for help from others. You don't have to do it all or do it all the time. There may be human and financial resources that you are unaware of that could lessen your burden as a caregiver. You will need to take periodic breaks for self-renewal. Going for lunch with a friend or taking a walk are simple, but vital, activities that can help you stay the course. Hospitals often sponsor support groups where caregivers can share experiences and understanding, and these, too, can make a tremendous difference if you are caring for an ailing loved one.

## The Future You

Finally, I want you to think back to when you imagined the future you coming back to tell you about retirement. How did your vision compare to the reality you have experienced? Would you have done anything differently, or were you happily surprised by the events that occurred?

I'd like you to try that exercise again. Imagine you, but five to ten years older than you are now, explaining that you've come from the future to give you the good news about your retirement. What is the retirement like that future you describes? Is it attainable, knowing everything you know now?

You can do the same with the other exercises and worksheets in this book. Whenever you need to check in and get back in touch with your original motivations for retirement, this book can be a useful resource.

Here's to late bloomers! You should be highly impressed with yourself and what you have been able to accomplish. I know you've put in quite a bit of work. This is just the beginning of an amazing phase in your life, one in which you achieve your goals and make the most of every day. You ignored the noise that said there was no chance for your retirement or that it was too late.

## JUST A FEW MORE THINGS TO DO . . .

- ☐ Continue to live the life you want in retirement.
- ☐ Work less.
- ☐ Earn just enough.
- ☐ Focus on being happier than ever.

### RESOURCES

Fidelity's Guide to Living in Retirement (www.fidelity.com/retirement-planning /plan-to-generate-income). Fidelity is a great resource for information, tools, and calculators to make sense of your investments. Even if you're not a customer, most of the learning center is free.

Root of Good (http://rootofgood.com/running-out-of-money-in-early-retirement/). This blog, written by and about a couple of early retirees, is a useful source of money saving and investing ideas. I like this particular link because it deals with contingencies.

"20 Ways to Stop Wasting Money and Start Saving Now" (www.refinery29.com /budgeting-tools-spending-diary#slide). This article does a nice job of combining personal (start by organizing clutter and cleaning out your wallet) with solid money-saving tips.

Acorns app (www.acorns.com). Make saving as easy as it gets with this handy app that rounds all your purchases up to the nearest dollar and invests the difference for you in a diversified portfolio.

Prepare to Care (assets.aarp.org/www.aarp.org_/articles/foundation/aa66r2_care.pdf). The AARP's guide for caregivers.

Assisted Living vs. Nursing Home (www.aplaceformom.com/senior-care-resources /articles/nursing-home-care). It's important to know how different retirement communities work, when deciding where you might be interested in living if you need to make that type of move in the future.

# You Rocked It

**Amazing!** Talk about getting serious when you need to be. You've completed the steps in this book to pull together a spot retirement plan that can provide for your needs and allow you to pursue the life you want to live.

I want you to feel supercharged, a big shot, a baller . . . whatever expression best describes being totally in charge and full of confidence. You can have a retirement that makes sense for you, one in which you work just a little, earn enough, and enjoy more. If you have goals left to meet or dreams you'd like to see fulfilled, today's retirement can provide you with the momentum you need to make things happen that you never had the guts to do. There's a freedom to retirement that many liken to being young again.

Yes, this retirement is different from the one your parents had. In some ways, it won't be as easy for you as it was for them. But they didn't have the opportunities available to you, the chance to sell your creativity and services to such a broad consumer market. They may have been able to bring in a few bucks renting out the guest house or knitting hats for people. You can keep the guest house rented by real tourists, whenever you want, and sell hats on Etsy as fast as you can make them. And within your first few years of retirement, there may be hundreds of new ways to earn income on the Internet. With the baby boomer population representing nearly 45 percent of the US workforce,[69] the market will invent new ways to tap the senior generation's resources.

Retirement may be a lot of fun, but it won't always be easy, especially during the early years. It's going to take effort to maintain your spending budget, stick to a withdrawal plan, and keep the income flowing. During the hard times, remember to reach out to family, friends, and the community for help. We are all in this new retirement reality together and your story is one that's becoming increasingly common.

Speaking of stories, I have to thank the 65 retirees from across the country who took the time to be surveyed for this book. I learned so much from your retirement stories, and I'm proud to know all of you. I don't know how I managed to find a random sampling of the most charitable, easygoing, relaxed, practical, and thrifty retirees around (I did get help from my retired mom, Linda, as well as retired friends, Mary and Susan, who passed the survey around to lots of retired friends. Thanks guys!) I was also surprised by how many of you had long-term care insurance. Maybe you are an especially practical bunch. Still, it gives me hope that it's not too late for the rest of us.

# Glossary

**401(K)**  An employer-sponsored retirement account. A 401(k) falls under the category of defined contribution plan, because the employee makes contributions for retirement from pre-tax salary. Investments held in a 401(k) are tax-deferred until the money is withdrawn at retirement. In some cases, the employer also makes contributions to the plan, often matching the employee's contributions up to a certain percentage. If you withdraw your money from a 401(k) plan before age 59½, you will likely pay a 10 percent penalty fee, plus federal tax and any applicable state and local income taxes.

**403(B)**  A tax-deferred retirement savings account offered to all employees of nonprofit or 501(c)(3) organizations, including public schools, hospitals, museums, churches, and charitable organizations. This account is similar to a 401(k) plan but for the nonprofit sector. Contributions are made from the employee's pre-tax salary, and invested to grow tax-deferred until you start to withdraw it at retirement, beginning at age 59½. As with 401(k) plans, if you withdraw your money before age 59½, you will pay a 10 percent penalty fee, plus federal tax and any applicable state and local income taxes. This is also known as a tax-sheltered annuity or TSA plan, because some 403(b) plans invest in annuity contracts. Many 403(b) plans offer a combination of mutual funds and annuities.

**ADVANCE HEALTH CARE DIRECTIVE**  A legal document that expresses your wishes for health care options, should you become incapacitated and unable to make decisions for yourself.

**ANGEL INVESTOR**  An individual or fund that invests in early-stage or start-up companies in exchange for equity shares. Sometimes known as "seed investors" or "friends and family investors," angels often provide the capital necessary to get the company off the ground.

**ANNUITY**  A contract in which an insurer agrees to make a series of income payments (either regularly or in a lump sum) in exchange for a premium paid by the investor.

**ASSET ALLOCATION**   A strategic mix of investments—stocks, bonds, and cash—designed to add diversification and reduce the risk of the portfolio as a whole.

**BEAR MARKET**   A period during which investors lose confidence and market prices decline by at least 20 percent for a period of two months or longer. Market declines that last for shorter periods of time, followed by periods when prices rise again, are known as corrections.

**BENEFICIARY**   A person or entity that stands to profit from something. The owner of a trust, will, insurance policy, or investment account, will name at least one beneficiary to receive the assets in the future.

**BONDS**   A debt offering made by a government, municipality, agency, or corporation that needs funding. It's like an I.O.U., promising to pay back the principal amount invested (also known as the face value of the bond) plus interest for the life of the bond. Because bonds provide periodic payments and return the principal when the bond matures, they are known as fixed-income investments. There are different types of bonds, with varying degrees of risk, depending on who issues them. Treasury bonds or US government debt is considered to be among the least risky, as it's backed by the full faith and credit of the US government. Corporate bonds are offered by companies looking to raise capital, and are either investment grade or high-yield (also known as junk bonds). Municipal or muni bonds are offered by states, cities, and local authorities to fund projects, and there are tax benefits for owning them.

**CAPITAL GAINS TAX**   A type of tax that's incurred when you sell an investment or other capital asset (real estate, land, art, etc.) at a price that's higher than what you paid for it. The capital gains tax rate depends on how long an investment is held: short-term capital gains are gains from investments owned for less than a year and they are taxed at the investor's ordinary income rate. Long-term capital gains are gains from investments held for a year or longer, and they are taxed at a much lower rate, which is between zero and 20 percent, depending on your income. Capital gains can be offset by capital losses, which are incurred when you sell an investment at a price that's lower than what you paid for it.

**CAPITAL INVESTMENT**   The funding needed for a company or enterprise to conduct business. Capital investment is typically achieved through equity or stock issuance, or debt or bond issuance.

**COST OF LIVING ADJUSTMENT (COLA)**   This is the adjustment that Social Security makes for inflation, not every year but each year in which inflation is said to have increased.

**DAY TRADING**   Buying and selling stock, foreign currencies, or other securities in the same day. Day traders differ from long-term investors because they are trying to capitalize on smaller, intra-day moves in the market. Successful day traders are typically very knowledgeable about the market and risk only capital they can afford to lose. However, some day traders use margins, or leverage, to increase the size and amounts of their trades. For this and other reasons, day trading can be a highly speculative and risky endeavor.

**DEFINED BENEFIT PLAN**   Sometimes called a traditional pension, a defined benefit plan is an employer-sponsored retirement plan in which the employer saves regularly for an employee's retirement. At retirement, a defined benefit plan provides a predetermined, fixed amount of income to the employee, based on a formula that factors in the employee's position, salary, and length of time at the company. The benefits are guaranteed by the employer as well as the Pension Benefit Guaranty Corp., a government agency designed to ensure pension plans meet their obligations in the private sector.

**DEFINED CONTRIBUTION PLAN**   An employer-sponsored retirement plan in which the employee, employer, or both make contributions for retirement. The benefits are based on the amount contributed to the plan and the performance of the investments within the plan. A 401(k) plan is a defined contribution plan.

**DIVIDENDS**   A dividend is a distribution of earnings from a company to its investors. Large, established companies often offer dividends to attract shareholders. This can increase the return of an investment that is no longer growing rapidly. Dividends can be paid out as income or reinvested as profit.

**EQUITIES**   Another way of describing a stock, which is essentially an equity share in the company. To invest in equities is to buy stocks, stock mutual funds, or stock exchange traded funds (ETFs).

**EXCHANGE TRADED FUND (ETF)**   A type of investment that represents a collection of securities. An ETF offers the broad exposure to different investments that you would find in a mutual fund, but it trades like a stock. That makes it easier for investors to buy and sell ETFs throughout the day. Most ETFs follow a specified index, such as the Standard & Poor's 500, the Dow Jones Industrials, or the NASDAQ. Because these investments often do not require the oversight of an investment manager, they tend to be less expensive than mutual fund counterparts.

**FIXED DEFERRED ANNUITY**   An annuity contract that makes fixed-rate payments for a set period of time. There are two phases to a deferred annuity: an accumulation phase and an income phase. Savings go into the annuity, income-tax deferred, during the accumulation period. The annuity makes fixed regular payments or a lump sum payment during the income phase. Annuities that have no accumulation phase and start to pay out within one year of paying the premium are known as immediate annuities.

**FUNDING ROUNDS**   The periods of phases in which companies attempt to raise capital for growth. These rounds typically begin with a seed round, which funds the early start-up costs. A series A round is designed to get investors excited about the development of a new product or service, even if there are still issues with the business. Venture capitalists often look to fund series A rounds of companies with potential. Series B rounds help finance growth, to expand the reach of the company. Series C funding and beyond is for successful businesses that have the potential to scale and become huge. Private equity investors and hedge funds are more likely to be involved in a series C funding round.

**HARD ASSETS**   Investments that have an intrinsic value. These include land and investment real estate, gold and silver, oil and gas, art and antiques. Hard assets are often tangible, meaning you can hold them in your hand.

**HEALTH CARE PROXY**   A person or entity who is legally allowed to make health decisions on your behalf should you become incapacitated.

**HEALTH SAVINGS ACCOUNT (HSA)**   A tax-favored medical savings account that accompanies a high-deductible health plan, meaning one that offers lower premiums each year but charges a high price if you become sick or hurt. An HSA is kind of like a 401(k) for medical costs. You make contributions that can be invested for tax-deferred growth. You don't have to use the assets this year and can often carry them over into retirement, which is a great cushion to have. If you are already saving in an HSA, keep doing it. But don't choose an HSA just to get the tax-deferred benefits. High-deductible health plans don't make sense for people who are older and more likely to need medical treatment. And if you really need the tax incentive to save, you can put funds into a Roth IRA for long-term medical costs.

**INDIVIDUAL RETIREMENT ACCOUNT (IRA)**   A type of investment account used by individuals to save for retirement. An IRA can be set up through a bank or mutual fund company and can be used to hold other retirement accounts when you leave a job. There are several types of IRAs, including traditional IRAs, Roth IRAs, SEP IRAs, and SIMPLE IRAs. Contributions to traditional IRAs may be tax deductible, depending on your income, and earnings are tax-deferred until retirement. Contributions made to Roth IRAs are not tax deductible, but earnings are generally tax-free at retirement. SIMPLE and SEP IRAs may be offered through small-business employers to allow employees to make contributions for retirement, and they are often used by self-employed retirement savers.

**INFLATION**   An increase in the prices of consumer goods and services over time, which can result in a decrease in the value of your money. In the United States, inflation is measured by the Consumer Price Index, which tracks changes in consumer prices of goods and services, and the Producer Price Index, which tracks selling prices.

**INTEREST**   The amount that a borrower is charged for a loan. If you are the borrower, through a loan or credit card, you pay an annual percentage rate based on the principal amount borrowed. This is also known as an interest rate. For investors, interest can represent the return on your investment or your share of ownership in the investment.

**MONEY MARKET FUND**   A short-term investment that allows for easy access and risk that is similar to cash.

**PENSION**   An employer-sponsored retirement plan. It is also known as a defined benefit plan, wherein the employer is responsible for funding a portion of the employee's retirement.

**PORTFOLIO**   A collection of investments owned by an individual, fund, or corporate entity. Your portfolio is made up of the different mutual funds, stocks, bonds, and other investments you hold.

**PORTFOLIO REBALANCING** Adjusting your investment holdings to fit your asset allocation target. The assets held in a portfolio should be weighted to fit your long-term goals and risk tolerance, for example 60 percent stocks, 35 percent bonds, 5 percent cash. This is called asset allocation, and it can get out of whack with big market swings. For example, if stocks rise, your stock portion may grow to represent 75 percent of your portfolio. Rebalancing involves buying and selling assets to maintain that original allocation.

**POWER OF ATTORNEY** A legal document giving someone the power to make decisions and take action on your behalf. Power of attorney for health care and financial decisions is known as durable power of attorney.

**PROBATE** The process, after an individual's death, wherein his or her will is legally validated.

**RETIREMENT ADMINISTRATOR** The person or company who is in charge of running your retirement plan. It could be your employer or an outside company that manages the plan. A retirement plan administrator should be identified in your plan document.

**ROLLOVER IRA** An individual retirement account that holds other tax-deferred investment accounts. If you want to take a 401(k) with you when you leave a job, you may be able to transfer it to a new employer's account. Otherwise, it makes sense to move the 401(k) into a rollover IRA. It's a tax-deferred investment account, and when your money is in it, you have access to all sorts of investments. You may like the choices you had in your 401(k), which is fine, but if you want more options, a rollover IRA can offer a broad range of options. And the investments continue to grow, tax deferred.

**SPOUSAL SOCIAL SECURITY BENEFITS** You are entitled to receive as much as 50 percent of the monthly benefits that your spouse receives on his or her record at full retirement age. If you have your own benefits, you will receive whichever is greater. If you are divorced, unmarried and not remarried, and your ex-spouse is entitled to receive benefits, you may be entitled to receive benefits on his or her record. If you are a widow or widower, you can receive full benefits as a survivor at full retirement age. You may be able to receive disability or other benefits earlier, so contact Social Security for more information: 800-772-1213 (TTY 800-325-0778).

**STANDARD & POOR'S 500 INDEX**   An index of 500 of the largest stocks in the US stock market, considered to be a measure of the broader market overall. Many mutual funds and ETFs use the S&P 500 Index as a benchmark to follow or compete against in trying to beat the market.

**SUCCESSOR TRUSTEE**   The person who assumes control of a trust once the initial trustee cannot.

**SWOT ANALYSIS**   A type of business analysis that identifies the internal strengths and weaknesses of a company, as well as external opportunities and threats. It's often presented in a grid. It can be used for strategic planning in building a company, or for management or improvement as a company grows.

**TAXABLE PORTFOLIO**   Investments held outside of a tax-favored retirement account, such as a 401(k) or IRA. Your taxable portfolio may include stocks, bonds, mutual funds, real estate, art and collectibles, and your checking and savings account.

**TRUSTEE**   A person or entity named to administer or oversee responsibility for assets that benefit another.

**TURNOVER RATES**   Portfolio turnover measures how frequently assets are bought and sold within a mutual fund. You can take the total amount of securities bought or sold over a given period (e.g., one year) and divide it by the net asset value (NAV) of the fund. A fund with a high turnover rate is likely to have higher transaction costs.

**VESTING**   The process through which an employee works a certain amount of time to receive a greater portion of benefits.

**WITHDRAW**   To take money out of an account. This could also be expressed as drawing from an account.

**WITHDRAWAL PLAN**   A strategy for pulling savings from your retirement accounts in a way that generates income for you and keeps the portfolio sustainable over a given period of years.

# Notes

1.  Helman, Ruth, Copeland, Craig, and Jack VanDerhi. "The 2015 Retirement Confidence Survey: Having a Retirement Savings Plan a Key Factor in Americans' Retirement Confidence." Employee Benefit Research Institute. *Issue Brief,* No. 413, April 2015. www.ebri.org/pdf/briefspdf/EBRI_IB_413 _Apr15_RCS-2015.pdf.

2.  Wang, Penelope. "The Real Reasons Americans Aren't Saving Enough for Retirement." *Money.* August 20, 2015. www.time.com/money/4003825 /real-reasons-not-saving-for-retirement/.

3.  Helman, Ruth, Copeland, Craig, and Jack VanDerhi. "The 2015 Retirement Confidence Survey: Having a Retirement Savings Plan a Key Factor in Americans' Retirement Confidence." Employee Benefit Research Institute. *Issue Brief,* No. 413, April 2015.

4.  "The Typical American Has This Much in Retirement Savings. How Do You Compare?" *The Motley Fool* (blog). October 9, 2015. www.fool.com/retirement /general/2015/01/10/the-typical-american-has-this-much-in-retirement-s.aspx

5.  Employee Benefit Research Institute. "FAQs about Benefits—Retirement Issues." Accessed February 26, 2016. www.ebri.org/publications/benfaq /index.cfm?fa=retfaq14.

6.  Center on Budget and Policy Priorities. "Policy Basics: 10 Facts about Social Security." Last modified August 13, 2015. www.cbpp.org/research /social-security/policy-basics-top-ten-facts-about-social-security.

7.  Drake, Bruce. "Number of Older Americans in the Workforce Is on the Rise." January 7, 2014. www.pewresearch.org/fact-tank/2014/01/07 /number-of-older-americans-in-the-workforce-is-on-the-rise/.

8.  Garver, Rob. "30 Percent of 'Retirees' Would Return to Labor Force." August 21, 2014. www.cnbc.com/2014/08/21/retirees-go-back-to-work.html.

9.  Berg, S. Z. "Growing Your Retirement Income Literally—by Farming." October 20, 2015. www.thestreet.com/story/13330012/1 /growing-your-retirement-income-literally-by-farming.html.

10. "About My Retirement Works." *My Retirement Works* (blog). Accessed February 26, 2016. myretirementworks.com/about/.

11. Block, Judie. *My Retirement Works* (blog). Accessed February 26, 2016. myretirementworks.com/road-to-retirement/#more-126

12. Eisenberg, Richard. "What Older Workers Want, but Aren't Getting." *Forbes.* April 2, 2014. www.forbes.com/sites/nextavenue/2014/04/02 /what-older-workers-want-but-arent-getting/#1a4af32f2499.

13. "Encore Careers: The Persistence of Purpose." Encore.org. 2014. Accessed February 27, 2016. www.encore.org/files/2014EncoreResearchOverview.pdf.

14. Achor, Shawn. *The Happiness Advantage.* New York: Crown Business, 2010.

15. Freidman, Howard, and Leslie R. Martin. *The Longevity Project.* New York: Penguin Books, 2011.

16. Robinson, John P. "Americans Less Rushed but No Happier: 1965–2010 Trends in Subjective Time and Happiness." *Social Indicators Research* 113, No. 3 (September 2013): 1091–1104.

17. Short, Kevin, ed. "Here Is the Income Level at Which Money Won't Make You Any Happier in Each State." *Huffington Business.* July 17, 2014. www.huffingtonpost.com/2014/07/17/map-happiness-benchmark_n_5592194.html.

18. Kushlev, Kostadin, Elizabeth W. Dunn, and Richard E. Lucas. "Higher Income is Associated with Less Daily Sadness but Not More Daily Happiness." *Social Psychology and Personality Science* 6, No. 5 (July 2015): 483–89. spp.sagepub.com/content/6/5/483.

19. Hamblin, James. "Buy Experiences, Not Things." *Atlantic.* October 7, 2014. www.theatlantic.com/business/archive/2014/10/buy-experiences/381132/

20. Blackman, Andrew. "Can Money Buy You Happiness?" *Wall Street Journal.* November 10, 2014. www.wsj.com/articles/can-money-buy-happiness-heres-what-science-has-to-say-1415569538.

21. "Study: Americans Get Happier with Age." *HuffPost Healthy Living.* August 12, 2011. www.huffingtonpost.com/2011/08/12/gallup-americans-happiest_n_925855.html#s328514title=Age_1824.

22. "Study Reveals Surprising Link between Age and Happiness." *Huff/Post 50.* February 12, 2014. www.huffingtonpost.com/2014/02/12/age-and-happiness_n_4773484.html.

23. Riggio, Ronald E., "Are You Psychologically Ready to Retire?" *Psychology Today.* January 9, 2015. www.psychologytoday.com/blog/cutting-edge-leadership/201501/are-you-psychologically-ready-retire.

24. Bell, Whitfield, and Leonard W. Labaree, eds. *Mr. Franklin: A Selection from His Personal Letters.* New Haven, CT: Yale University Press, 1956.

25. Birsel, Ayse. *Design the Life You Love.* New York: Ten Speed Press, 2015.

26. Kahn, Jennifer. "The Happiness Code." *New York Times Magazine.* January 14, 2016. www.nytimes.com/2016/01/17/magazine/the-happiness-code.html.

27. "20 Highest Paid Actors of Hollywood Like Robert Downey, Jr." *HuffPost Celebrity.* August 24, 2015. www.huffingtonpost.com/gobankingrates/20-highest-paid-actors-of_b_8032752.html; "Oprah Winfrey Net Worth." *The Richest* (blog). Accessed February 27, 2016. www.therichest.com/celebnetworth/celeb/media-mogul/oprah-winfrey-net-worth/.

28. blogs.cfainstitute.org/investor/2014/03/04/warren-buffetts -90-10-rule-of-thumb-for-retirement-investing/

29. "Social Security Benefit Amounts for the Surviving Spouse by Year of Birth." Official Social Security Website. Accessed February 27, 2016. www.socialsecurity.gov/planners/survivors/survivorchartred.html.

30. Morrissey, Monique. "Private-Sector Pension Coverage Fell by Half over Two Decades." *Economic Policy Institute Working Economics Blog.* January 11, 2013. www.epi.org/blog/private-sector-pension-coverage-decline/.

31. "Key Facts Regarding State and Local Government Defined Benefit Retirement Plans." Accessed February 27, 2016. www.nctr.org/pdf /PublicPensionKeyFacts.pdf.

32. The American College of Financial Services. "Crash Course Needed: Four Out of Five Americans Fail When Quizzed on How to Make Their Nest Eggs Last." December 3, 2014. www.theamericancollege.edu/ricp-retirement-income -survey/press-release.php.

33. Bengen, William P. "Determining Withdrawal Rates Using Historical Data." Accessed February 28, 2016. www.retailinvestor.org/pdf/Bengen1.pdf.

34. Mutual of America. "The Cost of a Mortgage." Accessed February 28, 2016. www.mutualofamerica.com/yrc/costofmortgage.

35. U.S. Department of Health and Human Services. "Who Needs Care?" Accessed February 28, 2016. longtermcare.gov/the-basics/who-needs-care.

36. American Health Insurance Plans. "Guide to Disability Income Insurance." Accessed February 29, 2016. www.nahu.org/consumer /PRO_113_14_GuidetoDI2013_F.pdf.

37. "Social Security Basic Facts." Official Social Security Website. October 13, 2015. www.ssa.gov/news/press/basicfact.html.

38. Powell, Robert. "The Secret to a Happier, Healthier Life: Just Retire." December 24, 2015. www.marketwatch.com/story/the-secret-to-a -happier-healthier-life-just-retire-2015-07-27.

39. "Fidelity Survey Finds While Boomers with Pensions More Likely to Retire at or before 65, Almost Half Will Retire with Debt," Business Wire. December 6, 2012. www.businesswire.com/news/home/20121206005754 /en/Fidelity%C2%AE-Survey-Finds-Boomers-Pensions-Retire-65.

40. Copeland, Craig. "Debt of the Elderly and Near Elderly, 1992–2013." Employee Benefit Research Institute. 36, No. 1 (January 2015). www.ebri.org/pdf /notespdf/EBRI_Notes.Jan15.Debt.pdf.

41. Federal Trade Commission. "Choosing a Credit Counselor." Consumer Information. November 2012. www.consumer.ftc.gov/articles /0153-choosing-credit-counselor.

42. Brandon, Emily. "7 Reasons Not to Move in Retirement." *U.S. News & World Report.* Money. January 21, 2014. money.usnews.com/money/retirement /articles/2014/01/21/7-reasons-not-to-move-in-retirement.

43. Graham, Carol. "Late-Life Work and Well-Being." Iza World of Labor. November 2014. timedotcom.files.wordpress.com/2015/01 /late-life-work-and-well-being-1.pdf.

44. www.bls.gov/opub/mlr/2013/article/labor-force-projections-to-2022-the -labor-force-participation-rate-continues-to-fall.htm

45. Holland, Kelley. "Why America's Campuses Are Going Gray." August 28, 2014. www.cnbc.com/2014/08/28/why-americas-campuses-are-going-gray.html.

46. Brandon, Emily. "How Retirees Can Attend College for Free." April 20, 2009. money.usnews.com/money/articles/2009/04/20 /forget-tuition-how-retirees-can-attend-college-for-free.

47. ibid.

48. Matos, Kenneth, and Ellen Galinsky. "2014 National Study of Employers." Society for Human Resource Management. Accessed February 29, 2016. familiesandwork.org/downloads/2014NationalStudyOfEmployers.pdf.

49. LaPonsie, Maryalene. "How Retirees Can Make Money in the Sharing Economy." August 20, 2015. money.usnews.com/money/retirement/articles /2015/08/20/how-retirees-can-make-money-in-the-sharing-economy.

50. Encore.org. "Ronald Stebenne." Accessed February 29, 2016. Encore.org/story /ronald-stebenne/.

51. Mulcahy, Diane. "Six Myths about Venture Capitalists." *Harvard Business Review*. May 2013. hbr.org/2013/05/six-myths-about-venture-capitalists.

52. AARP. "Phased Retirement and Flexible Retirement Arrangements: Strategies for Retaining Skilled Workers." Accessed February 29, 2016. assets.aarp.org /www.aarp.org_/articles/money/employers/phased_retirement.pdf.

53. Matthews, Ben. "Freelance Statistics 2015: The Freelance Economy in Numbers." *BenRMatthews* (blog). September 9, 2014. benrmatthews.com /freelance-statistics-2015/.

54. Fallon, Nicole. "In Most Countries, Freelancers Earn More Than Average Workers." *Business News Daily*. May 5, 2015. www.businessnewsdaily.com /7959-freelance-pay-rates.html.

55. Taylor, Mia. "How to Earn a Six-Figure Income in the Sharing Economy." *TheStreet* (blog). June 30, 2015. www.thestreet.com/story/13201387/1 /how-to-earn-a-six-figure-income-in-the-sharing-economy.html.

56. "1 in 3 Small Business Owners Are 65 or Older." *Small Business Labs* (blog). January 15, 2015. www.smallbizlabs.com/2015/01/1-in-3-small-business -owners-is-65-or-older.html

57. Beesley, Caron. "How to Estimate the Cost of Starting a Business from Scratch." SBA (US Small Business Administration). Last modified January 26, 2015. www.sba.gov/blogs/how-estimate-cost-starting-business-scratch.

58. www.fool.com/retirement/general/2016/02/06 /will-inflation-destroy-your-retirement-savings.aspx

59. DeGrace, Tom. "The Historical Rate of Return for the Stock Market Since 1900." StockPicksSystem. July 30, 2014. www.stockpickssystem.com /historical-rate-of-return/.

60. Bureau of Labor Statistics. Volunteering in the United States, 2015. US Department of Labor. February 25, 2016. www.bls.gov/news.release /volun.nr0.htm.

61. Widrich, Leo. "What Happens to Our Brains When We Exercise and How It Makes Us Happier." *Fast Company* (blog). February 4, 2014. www.fastcompany.com/3025957/work-smart/what-happens-to-our-brains -when-we-exercise-and-how-it-makes-us-happier.

62. Hamer, Mark, Kim L. Lavoie, and Simon L. Bacon. "Taking Up Physical Activity in Later Life and Healthy Ageing: The English Longitudinal Study of Ageing." *British Journal of Sports Medicine* 48, No. 3 (2014): 239–43. bjsm.bmj.com /content/48/3/239.

63. Lampit, Amit, Harry Hallock, and Michael Valenzuela. "Computerized Cognitive Training in Cognitively Healthy Older Adults: A Systematic Review and Meta-Analysis of Effect Modifiers." *PLOS Medicine.* December 17, 2014. journals.plos.org/plosmedicine/article?id=10.1371/journal.pmed.1001756.

64. Underwood, Emily. "Neuroscientists Speak out against Brain Game Hype." *Science.* October 22, 2014. www.sciencemag.org/news/2014/10 /neuroscientists-speak-out-against-brain-game-hype.

65. Kennedy, Vonnie. "Top 5 Dating Sites for Seniors." Senior Planet. February 8, 2013. seniorplanet.org/top-5-online-dating-sites-for-seniors/.

66. Heller, Steven. "Recalling the Craze for a Game of Chance." *New York Times* Arts Special. March 10, 2010. www.nytimes.com/2010/03/18/arts /artsspecial/18MAH.html?_r=0

67. Fidelity. "Six Strategies for Volatile Markets." January 15, 2016. www.fidelity.com/viewpoints/investing-ideas/strategies-for-volatile-markets.

68. AARP, Public Policy Institute. "Caregiving in the United States 2015." June 4, 2015. www.aarp.org/ppi/info-2015/caregiving-in-the-united-states-2015.html.

69. Fry, Richard. "Millenials Surpass Gen Xers as the Largest Generation in the U.S. Labor Force." PewResearchCenter. May 11, 2015. www.pewresearch.org /fact-tank/2015/05/11/millennials-surpass-gen-xers-as-the-largest- generation-in-u-s-labor-force/.

# Index

CPSIA information can be obtained
at www.ICGtesting.com
Printed in the USA
BVOW07s1844230416

445021BV00003B/4/P